NATURAL MAGIC

Oxford University Press, Amen House, London E.C.4

GLASGOW NEW YORK TORONTO MELBOURNE WELLINGTON
BOMBAY CALCUTTA MADRAS KARACHI LAHORE DACCA
CAPE TOWN SALISBURY NAIROBI IBADAN ACCRA
KUALA LUMPUR HONG KONG

NATURAL MAGIC

*Studies in the Presentation of
Nature in English Poetry
from Spenser to Marvell*

KITTY W. SCOULAR

OXFORD
AT THE CLARENDON PRESS
1965

TO MY
MOTHER AND FATHER

*When your possessions are small
you enlarge them with wonder*

PREFACE

I HAVE attempted to do two things in this book, to describe some aspects of European sensibility in its responses to the natural world during the sixteenth and seventeenth centuries, and to assemble several English poems of the period with the kind of annotation which relates them to contemporary currents of taste.

The Renaissance poet did not write from a naked mind, but from an informed one, aware of poetic traditions to which he must perforce have some relation, whether in his continuity of certain themes and his expansion upon their possibilities, or in his critical reply to their manner and attitudes. The writing of poems about the natural world presupposed a cultivated audience who would appreciate a skilful rearrangement of old commonplaces to make new poems.

The selection of poems has been made as representative as possible of the different ways of writing about the natural world during the chosen period. So I have included a brief personal poem of an epistolary sort, a poem of general reflection on the universe, some parts of a georgic, an abbreviated version of a light mythological narrative, a verse-fable, a battle of birds, the hyperbolic praise of a creature, a contemplative landscape-poem, and an estate-poem. Marvell's poem, "Upon Appleton House, To my Lord *Fairfax*", I have found sufficiently interesting to give it a fuller commentary. Subsidiary notes accompany the text of this poem which, though more easily available, in H. M. Margoliouth's indispensable edition of *The Poems & Letters*, than other poems included, is given as a fitting accompaniment to the section devoted to it. For the text of the Lovelace poems included I have followed C. H. Wilkinson's edition.

I should particularly like to acknowledge the continual guidance and encouragement given me by Mr. J. B. Leishman. Miss Ethel Seaton, Miss Helen Gardner, Miss K. M. Lea, and Professor James Kinsley have offered me valuable suggestions and criticism at different stages in the growth of this book. Among friends I owe a special debt to Dr. Alastair Fowler, and to the late James Smart for help with Southwell's text; but many others have shared in this book by their sustained interest and in random other ways. Without financial assistance from the University of Edinburgh and the West Lothian Educational Trust I should have been unable to undertake research. I should also like to thank the staff of St. Hugh's College Library, Oxford, the National Library of Scotland, Edinburgh University Library, and the British Museum for the privilege of consulting books. Above all, to the staff of the Bodleian Library is due my appreciation of their unstinted help over a long period.

Scottish Church College
Calcutta, 1958.

CONTENTS

LIST OF PLATES

With the exception of Nos. VIII and IX, the plates are reproduced from copies in the Bodleian Library, Oxford, by permission of the Curators.

IN THE TEXT

1 · NATURAL MAGIC

—◄-◄-◄·⚬⚬⚬·⭤-►-►►—

The Complete Gentleman

HENRY PEACHAM (1578?–1642?) first engaged in educating the complete gentleman at the grammar school of Wymondham in Norfolk, not far from Barnham Broome, where the family manor of his pupil Edward Chamberlaine was situated. He had an eye on the Court, and presented two emblem-books in manuscript to the King and his son. 'To my towardly and hopefull Scholar Maister Edward Chamberlaine, of Barnham Broome' appeared in *Thalia's Banquet* (1620), a collection of poems by Peacham. A related group of interests is indicated by his other writings, *The Art of Drawing with the Pen* (1606), enlarged as *Graphice* (1612), an emblem book, *Minerva Britanna* (1612), and *The Compleat Gentleman* (1622).

NED, never looke again those daies to see,
Thou liv'st, when thou appliedst thy booke with me,
What true affection bare we each to either,
How often walking in the fields together:
Have I in Latin giv'n the names to thee,
Of this wild Flower, that bent, this blossom'd tree,
This speckled Flie, that Hearb, this water rush,
This worme, or weed, the Bird on yonder bush?
How often when yee have beene ask'd a play,
With voices viols have we pass'd the day,
Now entertaining these weake aires of mine,
Anon the deepe delicious Transalpine,[1]
Another while with pencill or with pen,
Have limnd or drawn our friends pourtraies; and then
Commixing many colours into one,
Have imitated some carnation,
Strange field-found flower, or a rare seene flie,

[1] *Musica Transalpina* (1588) Nicholas Yonge's madrigal-book.

B

A curious land-schap or a clouded sky?
Then haply wearie of all these would goe,
Unto that Poeme[1] I have labourd so:
Thus past our leasureable howers away;
And yee did learne even in the midst of play.

Bounty

JOHN HAGTHORPE (fl. 1627) was a Yorkshire poet before Marvell, and in *Divine Meditations, and Elegies* (1622), which have Creation as their chief subject, his manner is sometimes not unlike Herbert's.

FOR Gods most compleate bountie not content
With such a single liberalitie,
Therefore this great varietie hath lent;
As much abhorring poore vacuitie
And indigence, in all his workes divine,
Which all with compleat bounteous fulnes shine.

The Rivers and the Seas be full of fish;
The earth is full of trees, of grasse, of plants,
And full of creatures fram'd to feed on this;
The ayre is full of her inhabitants.
All things on earth doe of this fulnes share;
No emptie place: all fild with vitall ayre.

But man may sooner loose himselfe in quest,
And survey of these blessings manifold,
Much sooner, then discover in the least,
The severall gifts and vertues that they hold:
For in the least so many worths we find,
As much surmount mans weak sin darkned mind.

How many severall gifts hath the *Maguayze*?[2]
How many hath *Maldivars*[3] fruitfull tree?

---

[1] 'A second volume of Emblemes, done into Latine verse with their pictures', that is, one of the Royal manuscripts.
[2] The Canary Islands.
[3] The Maldive Islands in the Indian Ocean, famed for their coconuts.

Which are as foyles to beautifie, and praise
Our plenties infinite varietie?
One tree doth them with all abundance store,
And sweet content, and all ours can no more.

Yet here with us some one thing seeme to stand
In stead of thousands: As the Sheepe and Cow.
This brings the Oxe, that tills and fats the land,
That warmely clothes us. This our feete doth shoo,
And with their flesh and milke the most are fed,
But milk's the poore mans Phisick, meat, drink, bread.

And why's this fulnes? for this end alone,
That Man for fulnes of things naturall,
Should returne fulnesse in affection;
Fulnesse of *Love* and Grace spirituall:
For if in these there be vacuitie,
True Motion, Essence, Light, Life none can be.[1]

John Hagthorpe, *Divine Meditations, and Elegies*, 1622.

I

A poet may in the dryest age call his contemporaries to an attitude of wonder; but when his society is already inclined to approach religion, the arts, and natural philosophy with an expectation of being offered the sensational and the arcane, he is at the beck and call of their anticipations, and wonder itself is tied to certain conventions. Some particular strengths and weaknesses of the poetry which appeared in England during the time within which Spenser and Marvell wrote and published are related to this fact. The poet, as so many of his apologists emphasized, was independent of the normal course of the world; but in an age when Nature herself often seemed to depart from her normal course, it was legitimate for the poet to follow her into her by-ways, to imitate 'Chance's better

[1] Hagthorpe follows theAristotelian doctrine that there is no empty space in the universe, 'si enim ulla sit vacuitas in affectibus, non est vera motus, essentia, visio, vita'.

Wit'. So the poet was in the paradoxical position of being both free from the ordinary pattern of things, and committed to a pattern of marvels.

The term 'natural magic' had a varied history before it entered more recent usage by way of Arnold's estimate of Keats. During the sixteenth century it stood as a descriptive term on the borderline between a mystical Paracelsan alchemy involving a supposed communion with the hidden forces of nature, and a more modern conception of scientific effort. As a recent historian of the subject has demonstrated,[1] the suspicion of magic among the early Fathers of the Church gave place gradually to the acceptance of a 'natural magic' which was lawful and distinct from the evil practices of the necromancers, 'the application of true and natural causes to produce rare and unusual effects by methods not superstitious or diabolical'.[2] The scope of natural magic was variously defined. To Pico della Mirandola in his youth it was a power over the hidden forces of nature, giving apparently miraculous results and uniting any 'virtue in the earth or sky'.[3] To Jerome Cardan, as he made known in his books De Rerum Varietate (1557) and De Subtilitate Rerum (1550), it was knowledge of the principles of sympathy and antipathy among things.[4] English interest in this branch of the occult is indicated by the translation of G. B. della Porta's Magiae Naturalis Libri IV (1558),[5] a book combining accounts of natural marvels, mostly untrue, with instructions for the production of illusions, new species of plants, and other small miracles. Sir Thomas Browne read Gaspar Schott's Magia Universalis Naturae et Artis (1657–9) and Cardan, and Thomas Heywood knew Hercules Strozza's Libri de Naturale Magia.[6] To others natural magic was closer to the harnessing of nature for the practical benefit of mankind.[7] This was the attitude of Bacon,

---

[1] Lynn Thorndike, A History of Magic and Experimental Science (Columbia, 1923–41). See also C. S. Lewis, English Literature in the Sixteenth Century (Oxford, 1954), pp. 2–14.
[2] Thorndike, op. cit. vi. 415.　　　　[3] Ibid. iv. 495.
[4] Ibid. v. 571.
[5] Translated by T. Young and S. Speed, as Natural Magick (1658).
[6] The Hierarchie of the blessed Angells (1635), p. 214.
[7] Thorndike, op. cit. vi. 377; F. Piccolomineus, Librorum ad scientiam de natura (1596).

who wished to rescue the term from the disciples of Paracelsus and apply it to the works of reason rather than imagination.[1] Their claim, as he saw it, was to make science usurp the place of religion, rather than allowing it to seek its own ends by the appropriate means. The term also had a somewhat lighter definition, in the sense of conjuring-tricks, the practice of a harmless sort of deception, and the construction of mechanical ingenuities, such as are described by della Porta, Schott, and Bishop Wilkins in his *Mathematicall Magick* (1648). It was Bacon especially who wished to free the term from triviality on the one hand, from an over-attention to nature's jokes and surprises, and from extravagant and unreal claims on the other.

For weal or for woe, the poet of the period was also inclined to shift off in the direction of extravagance or triviality, and in so doing to avoid that central and recreative humanity and meaningful independence by which poetry thrives. Only, unlike the scientist, the poet may shelter both mystery and ingenuity under his roof without harming his work, so long as it is not possessed absolutely by one or the other, to become excessively obscure or trite or affected, losing a genuine sense of wonder in the pursuit of a false sort of necromancy with its own spurious surprises, the repetition of formulas, or the conjuration of marvels for their own sake.

For the poet of our period and his society, wonder was a habit of mind knitting together an awareness and appreciation of the variety, the mystery, and the flux of the universe. *Variety, enigma, metamorphosis* were terms which might describe either the arts or the natural world,[2] the abundance of forms in the universe was matched with a copious style, its enigmatic quality with the riddle, the allegory, the hard metaphor, and its changeability with a style transmuting one thing into another. Nor were these three qualities regarded as mutually

---

[1] *The Advancement of Learning* (1605), book ii, fols. 33^r, 46^r.

[2] See H. S. Wilson, 'Some Meanings of "Nature" in Renaissance Literary Theory', *Journal of the History of Ideas*, ii (1941), 430–48; H. V. S. Ogden, 'The Principles of Variety and Contrast in Seventeenth Century Aesthetics, and Milton's Poetry', ibid. x (1949), 159–82; Joseph A. Mazzeo, 'Universal Analogy and the Culture of the Renaissance', ibid. xv (1954), 299–304.

exclusive, either in nature or in literature; rather did they con-
verge upon one another.[1] The variety of the universe and its
mystery were closely connected with its fluctuations. The kinds
of poem which tended to be most popular were mirrors of
these qualities. 'Poesy', wrote Bacon, 'cheereth and refresheth
the soul, chanting things rare and various, and full of vicissi-
tudes.' The long poem was an opportunity for reflecting the
varieties of the universe both in structure and in content, and
particularly in its descriptions and expanded similes. Among
shorter poems, a predilection for tales of metamorphosis, for
parable and symbol and emblem are strong enough evidence
of a taste for transformation and enigmatic obscurity. And in
the closer texture of poetry, in its diction and favourite figures,
the same three qualities were often prominent.

Even new scientific discoveries were new opportunities for
the poet to extend his own empire. For the practical scientists
new instruments were primarily improved means towards
more accurate measurement and observation; for the poets,
they were emblems. And the scientists themselves, regarding
them imaginatively, might interpret them in that way. The
burning glass might suggest the concentration of the Light of
Lights in small space, the prism the colourful transformation
of the common, and the microscope and telescope the insight
of faith.[2]

As it is in the works of *Nature*, where there are many common
things of excellent beauty, which for their *littlenesse* do not fall under
our sence; they that have experimented the use of *Micrescopes*, can
tell, how in the parts of the most minute creatures, there may be
discerned such gildings and embroderies, and such curious varietie
as another would scarce beleive. . . . So it is likewise in *the wayes of
Providence*, those designes that in respect of our apprehensions are
carried on by a crypticall involved method, are yet in themselves

---

[1] See Randle Cotgrave's *Dictionarie of the French and English Tongues* (1611),
Variété: 'varietie, change, choice, diversitie; ficklenesse, inconstancie, mutabilitie', and
Dr. Johnson's illustrations from our period of *Variety* in its first meaning: 'Change;
succession of one thing to another; intermixture of one thing with another.'

[2] See Robert Boyle, *Occasional Reflections upon Several Subjects* (1665), 'Discourse
Touching Occasional Meditations', pp. 30, 36; and Section III, Reflection x; Section VI,
Reflection viii.

of as excellent contrivance, as any of those, that seem to be of more
facile and perspicuous order.[1]

The 'Spectacles of *Faith*',[2] 'the perspective glass of Faith'[3] had
already revealed much that was unusual about the universe.
Now new discoveries illuminated the truth of old ideas, and
extended the awareness of variety and vastness, mystery and
impermanence.

For there are secrets and mysteries of two kindes, as the Schoole
presents them; some things are so, *Quia quaedam interposita*. Because
though the thing be near enough unto me, yet somthing is interposed between me, and it, and so I cannot see it: And some things
are so, *Quia longe seposita*, because they are at so remote a distance,
as that, though nothing be interposed, yet my sight cannot extend
to them.[4]

> *Nature*, who with like *State*, and equal *Pride*,
> Her *Great Works* does in *Height* and *Distance* hide,
> And shuts up her *Minuter Bodies* all
> In curious frames, *imperceptibly small*.
> Thus still *incognito*, she seeks *Recess*
> In Greatness *half-seen*, or *dimme* Littleness.[5]

The word *wonder* possesses several shades of meaning. For
Aristotle, it was a necessary stage on the way to learning,[6]
'curiosity' in one of its modern senses, 'the seede of knowledge',
as Bacon described it.[7] In this sense, the state of wonder could
be equated with the state of ignorance. Both for Bacon and for
the satirist Samuel Butler this was the most important sense, a
condition of mind only temporary and immature and to be
abandoned as soon as possible, though to Butler the Royal
Society had not yet shed it.

  [1] John Wilkins, *A Discourse concerning the Beauty of Providence in all the rugged passages of it* (1649), pp. 49, 68–69.
  [2] Joshua Sylvester, *Du Bartas his Divine Weekes and Workes* (5th ed. 1621), p. 5.
  [3] Christopher Harvey, *The Synagogue* (1640), 'Engines'; Henry Vaughan, *Silex Scintillans* (1650), 'They are all gone into the world of light'.
  [4] *The Sermons of John Donne*, ed. G. R. Potter and E. M. Simpson, Univ. of California Press, vii. 98.
  [5] Richard Leigh, *Poems upon several Occasions* (1675), ed. Hugh Macdonald (Oxford, 1947), pp. 22–23, 'Greatness in Little'.
  [6] *Opera*, 982^{b}12, 1371^{a}32–33.
  [7] *The Advancement of Learning* (1605), book i, fol. 5^v.

When all the rest began t'admire,
And, like a Train, from him took Fire,
Surpriz'd with Wonder, beforehand,
At what they did not understand,
Cry'd out, impatient to know what
The Matter was, they wonder'd at.[1]

Aristotle had also described nature's intricate and beautiful forms as wonderful.[2] Here wonder was rather connected with aesthetic appreciation. No one was more aware than Bacon of the confusion of scientific and literary attitudes which existed in his day. Natural history, he wrote, had been 'curious in nothing but the variety of things';[3] it had been deflected from observation of the central operations of the universe to its jokes, rarities, and miracles. And although he knew well and quoted from Aristotle's dicta on the craftsmanship of nature, even in its minutest forms,[4] he did not show himself enthusiastic about that aspect of her intricacies. If he wished men to apply themselves to study them, it was to discover what laws governed their operations, and not merely to admire.[5] As a controlling attitude of mind, admiration was unpractical, because it depended on sudden insights rather than on slow and patient examination.[6] Such terms as *stupified*, *astounded*, *bewitched*, and *mystery* were not among the compliments in Bacon's vocabulary describing the scientific attitude. Nor did he wish his contemporaries to be satisfied with their present awareness of the universe. The proper scientific attitude to nature's varieties was to be a respectful watching of her changes. For he recognized the world to be a much subtler and more complex place than most people realized. The word *subtilty* is a significant favourite of his, indicating a complexity to be penetrated and interpreted by all possible legitimate means. The universe is the riddle given to man for his solution by the observation of its processes, and the office of the scientist is to bring about change through the exercise of his art.

---

[1] Samuel Butler, *Satires and Miscellaneous Poetry and Prose*, ed. R. Lamar (Cambridge, 1928), p. 4: 'The Elephant in the Moon'.   [2] *De partibus animalium*, 645ᵃ.
[3] *Novum Organum* (1620), II. xxvii.   [4] Aristotle, *Opera*, 847ᵃ.
[5] *Novum Organum*, I. lxxxv.   [6] Ibid. xlvii.

Yet Bacon preserved wonder for poetry and for faith. If imagination and invention, fable and myth and miracle were to be separated from scientific study, they had still their proper area of operation. Wonder might be only the initial stage in the pursuit of scientific truth; in worship it was central, where the acknowledgement of human ignorance was appropriate to the humility of men before their Maker. '. . . for the contemplation of Gods Creatures and works produceth (having regard to the works and creatures themselves) knowledge, but having regard to God, no perfect knowledge, but wonder, which is broken knowledge.'[1] Scientifically considered, the creatures were worthy of correct description (so many emblems were spoiled by being based on inaccurate natural history), but considered as the works of God, they might still be surrounded by an inexplicable mystery. Some writers were more inclined than others to suggest that divine truth in good measure might be gathered from the creatures, that 'every beast is a natural vision, which we ought to see and understand, for the more cleare apprehension of the invisible Majesty of God'.[2] Others were more 'content to wonder, in silence'.[3]

Then apart from the normal course of nature, which in itself was bound to draw admiration, there was the possibility of miracle, the definition of which sometimes turned on the attitude it induced in its witnesses. 'The word *Miraculum*', wrote Thomas Heywood in 1635, 'importeth a thing moving stupor and admiration; for those which behold a Miracle, stand amased, as confounded at the effects, when they cannot apprehend the causes. Or else it is a thing, which from whence it comes, or by what meanes, passeth apprehension: for whatsoever happeneth beyond the course of Nature begetteth admiration.'[4]

Wonder was also preserved for poetry through the unique operation of the imagination, whose special privilege it was

[1] *The Advancement of Learning*, ed. cit., book i, fol. 6ʳ.
[2] Edward Topsell, *The Historie of Four-Footed Beastes* (1607), sig. A4ᵛ, 'The Epistle Dedicatory'.
[3] Joseph Hall, *Works* (1647), p. 317.
[4] Thomas Heywood, *The Hierarchie*, p. 306.

to contradict expectation and normality, to combine where reason and observation separated, to bound the world in a moment. Most frequently the idea of the special comprehensive powers of the soul was presented without philosophical refinement; but its neo-Platonic basis might be made apparent. Since there is 'nothing in this world, but hath a conformity, resemblance or relation, with other, though the subjects be more or lesse unlike',[1] the poet is at liberty to find these resemblances, 'to roam above the Universe, and return home laden with rich, but far fetch'd Conceits',[2] a prerogative which was being denied to him at the turn of the eighteenth century.

It was a precarious balance that was achieved by Bacon, by the separation of one human activity from another. A little shift, and the natural sciences might become unrealistic, or poetry itself might be governed by their standards of truth to fact. That science did not keep the balance has already been suggested: hence the cult of the virtuoso during the seventeenth century, the dabbler in experimentation for aesthetic motives.[3]

During our period, however, the qualities of variety, mystery, and novelty were preserved among the insights of a wonder which was closer to religious awe and to enjoyment of the arts than to scientific curiosity at its purest. Even Aristotle was interpreted optimistically as a pious theist: his delight in beautiful creatures might be transformed to suggest his recognition of miracles: '. . . wee reade a continuall Lecture of the Wisedome of the Almightie Creator, by beholding even in the feather of the *Peacocke* a Miracle, as *Aristotle* saith.'[4]

A habit of wonder is the natural outcome of a contemplative

[1] Henri Estienne, *L'Art de faire les devises* (Paris, 1645), translated by Thomas Blount as *The Art of Making Devises* (1646), pp. 37–38.

[2] *The Critical Works of John Dennis*, ed. E. N. Hooker (Baltimore, 1939, 2 vols.), i, p. 2, 'Preface to *The Passion of Byblis*' (1692). See Joshua Poole, *The English Parnassus* (1657), under *Admire, Admirable, Amazed, Astonisht, Beautifull, Fancy* ('striding from the Center to the Circumference of the world, by a kind of omnipotency creating and annihilating things in a moment, and marrying things divorced in nature'), *Impossible, Incredible, Never*.

[3] Walter E. Houghton, Jr., 'The English Virtuoso in the Seventeenth Century', *J.H.I.* iii (1942), 51–73, 190–219.

[4] Henry Peacham, *The Compleat Gentleman* (3rd ed., 1634), p. 125.

attitude to life which became increasingly familiar to English
readers of the sixteenth and seventeenth centuries.[1] 'The minde
of man, which delights in nothing so much as in mysteries,
may make whole nature a ceremony, and all the creatures tipes
and resemblances of spirituall things.'[2] On the one hand, there
was a multiplying output of emblem literature to popularize
this kind of piety;[3] on the other hand, there was a spread of the
belief that the countryman, separated from the contaminating
influences of city life, was better able to practise contemplation
than the townsman.[4] Books of devotion began to appear with
titles like *A Divine Herball*, or *Meditations from the Creatures*,
The Creatures Praising God, or *The Spirituall Use of an Orchard*;[5]
nor did books of natural history, which had for long tended
to include emblematic and moral instructions among their
material, lose their own particular blend of piety. The titles of
Edward Topsell's collections betray his primary interest: they
are intended to be 'Necessary for all Divines and Students,
because the Story of every Beast is amplified with Narrations
out of Scriptures, Fathers, Phylosophers, Physitians, and Poets:
wherein are declared divers Hyeroglyphicks, Emblems, Epigrams'.[6] In his *Historie of Four-Footed Beastes* he explained that

[1] R. C. Wallerstein, *Studies in Seventeenth Century Poetic* (Wisconsin, 1950), chap.
viii; Louis Martz, *The Poetry of Meditation* (1954).

[2] Godfrey Goodman, *The Fall of Man, or the corruption of Nature* (1616), p. 153.

[3] Mario Praz, *Studies in Seventeenth-Century Imagery* (1939); Rosemary Freeman,
English Emblem Books (1948).

[4] See the continental anthologies of classical and modern writers, *Aulica Vita, Et
opposita huic Vita Privata*, ed. Henricus Petreus-Herdesianus (2nd ed., Frankfurt, 1578),
De Re Rustica, ed. Joachim Camerarius (Nuremberg, 1577, also 1583, 1596), *Amphitheatrum Sapientiae Socraticae Joco-seriae*, ed. Caspar Dornavius (Nuremberg, 1619),
pp. 781–815, 'Vita rustica', 'Vita solitaria'.

In England, see Roger Baynes (1577), Conrad Heresbach,
Foure Bookes of Husbandry, Newely Englished . . . by B. Googe (1577, six eds. till 1631),
Sir John Harington, *The Prayse of Private Life*, based on Petrarch's *De vita solitaria*
(first printed from MS., *The Letters and Epigrams of Sir J. Harington*, ed. N. E. McClure,
Philadelphia, 1930). Contrast English versions of Guevara, *De vitae rusticae prae aulica
vita commodis* (1542), by Sir Fraunces Briant (1548) and Henry Vaughan (1651).

[5] Thomas Adams (1610); Thomas Taylor (1628, 1629, 1632); Godfrey Goodman
(1622, 1624); Ralph Austen (1653). Compare Thomas Dekker, *Four birds of Noahs
arke* (1609), M. A. Symson, *Heptameron, The Seven Dayes, That is, Meditations and
Prayers, Upon the worke of the Lords Creation* (Saint Andrews, 1621). See also Helen C.
White, *English Devotional Literature [Prose] 1600–1640* (University of Wisconsin
Studies, no. 29, 1931), pp. 179–80, 212–14, 243, 264.

[6] *The Historie of Four-Footed Beastes*, the title-page.

the uses of the creatures were not only practical, in the pro-
vision of food, clothing, and medicine for man, but moral
and religious. By their creation man has been made aware of
God's power and providence. By their use in worship as sacri-
ficial symbols, and in contemplation as fragmentary reminders
of the divine, as examples for imitation or warning, he has
been made aware of his salvation and his duty. Topsell stood
uncritically and with a tendency to pedantry within a long
tradition of Christian devotion, and his ways of making the
creatures his preceptors are comparable with such earlier
systematizations as Hugh of St. Victor's 'De quatuor modis
exeundi per contemplationem'.[1] For him, reflection upon the
creatures reminds men that life is brief, yet it also offers a
limited insight into the divine. They may be considered as
ministers to human need, or as images of human vice and
virtue. Since the modern reader is bound to accept the Baconian
criticism that the unshifting and fixed emblematic meanings
given to the creatures were not really inherent in them, but
were human inventions, subject to correction according to
observable fact, his own admiration will rather be directed
towards the strength of the original piety which was determined
to see the value of every part of creation within the theological-
ethical framework of its faith, and towards the considerable
intellectual versatility which produced such wisdom from
material so frequently unpromising. Far from stanching crea-
tivity during our period, the inheritance of wonders encouraged
the production of more, and the habit of free contemplation
released the mind to find even further astonishing significances
in things ordinary or more remote.

If any single English writer was responsible for popularizing
the contemplation of the creatures as a religious exercise, it
was probably Joseph Hall, Bishop of Exeter.[2] Besides encourag-
ing retirement for study and devotion in his private correspondence, he wrote *The Arte of Divine Meditation* (1606)[3]

---

[1] Migne, *Patrologiae Latinae*, clxxvi. 637–8.
[2] H. Fisch, 'Bishop Hall's Meditations', *Review of English Studies*, xxv (1949), 210–21.
[3] There were later editions, 1607, 1609, 1634.

giving advice about the procedure of contemplation. Of the two kinds of meditation which he discussed, it was the first, 'Meditation Extemporall', which applied more closely to the creatures, while the second and more complicated method was applicable rather to Biblical and theological subjects. Yet the pattern which can be distinguished in the nineteen divisions of the set meditation is a simple one, beginning with the minute consideration of a subject, continuing with the drawing of devout reflections from the different features of the subject, and ending with the movement of the affections in worship and resolve. Since the end of meditation is purification of the mind and will, he reminded his readers to avoid obscurities of thought and too literal an adherence to method. Extemporal meditation did not need time or place, and its subjects were the matters of ordinary observation of a man about his daily occupations.

Of Extemporall Meditation there may be much use, no rule: forasmuch as our conceits herein vary according to the infinite multitude of objects, and their divers manner of preferring themselves to the mind; as also for the suddennesse of this act . . . The creatures are half lost, if we only employ them, not learn something of them. God is wronged, if his creatures be unregarded: ourselves most of all, if we read this great volume of the creatures, and take out no lesson for our instruction.[1]

This was the kind of meditation of which Hall gave abundance of examples in his *Occasional Meditations* (1630),[2] drawn partly from the life of affairs, but mainly from the observations of animals and insects, of weather and of landscape. The simplified pattern, with its three steps, is usually present, first observation, then application, then wish or prayer; and wonder, both as a word and as an attitude, is never very far away. 'The less I can know, O Lord, the more let me wonder; and the less I can satisfy myself with marvelling at thy works, the more let me adore the majesty and omnipotence of thee, that wroughtest them.'[3]

[1] Op. cit., chap. iii.
[2] Also 1631, and enlarged, 1633.
[3] *The Breathings of the Devout Soul* (1648), xix.

There is a particular way of regarding man's relation with the
world which unites Hall with many of his contemporaries.
The lordship of the universe, which was lost at the Fall, may
be recovered in a life of Christian devotion, by a moderate and
joyful use of God's creatures, and a recognition that spiritual
instructions may be drawn from them. This is the outlook of
Donne, discoursing on the renewal of unity between body and
soul, even in this life, which accompanies a spiritual resurrection, as a shadow of the final resurrection.[1] It is the outlook of
Jeremy Taylor, teaching the practice of God's presence at all
times, which results in the transformation of the ordinary into
signposts of the divine through prayer and short devotions
throughout the night and day.[2] Traherne's *Centuries of Meditation* are a sharply distinct and impassioned presentation of an
attitude which informed much instruction in piety during the
seventeenth century, though he gave an easier acceptance than
some to both sides of the paradox that the world as man's is
unredeemed, yet as God's is to be highly valued.

For because His love is free, so are His treasures. He therefore
that will despise them because he hath them is marvellously irrational:
the way to possess them is to esteem them. And the true way of
reigning over them, is to break the world all into parts, to examine
them asunder.[3]

The habit of meditation on the very course of life brought to
the formality of the emblem a personal tone. The moral lessons
and spiritual types that previously were shut up within literary
confines were now to be sought not only in books but in the
stuff of life itself. The realistic use of the first person was in this
way introduced into the poetry of contemplation, and a
dramatic sense of place also.

That Hall's attitude and practice were not parochial but
common to Christian Europe is suggested by a comparison of
some of his writings with the prose romance of the Spanish
writer, Baltasar Gracian, *El Criticon* (1650-3), translated into

---

[1] *Sermons*, ed. cit. vii, no. 3, especially pp. 103-4.
[2] *Holy Living and Holy Dying* (1650).
[3] *Centuries of Meditation*, ed. B. Dobell (1908), I. xxiii.

English by Sir Paul Rycaut as *The Critick* (1681). The hero of
the romance is Andrenio, who lived in a cave and was nurtured
by animals until maturity, when he suddenly emerged and saw
the outside world for the first time, realizing its flux as no man
since Adam had been able to do.[1] At first each phenomenon
appeared before his eyes with the value of an unrepeatable
event: the rising of the sun he believed to be a unique happen-
ing until the dawn of the second day. Through Andrenio,
Graçian enunciated clearly the idea that it is the uniqueness,
the separateness of each event and creature which is the source
of wonder, and so of worship. If the world were stable, it
would please for only a short time, 'but instead of this, it has
a form changing night and day, for ever displaying a new sky
and new beauties. It never tires me in my observations, but
presents as many varieties as there are stars, with a solemn and
unpredictable confusion that draws our awe. It is a natural
enigma of the Almighty, only understood by the wise.'[2] Hall
in his *Contemplations* also considered the light which 'was by
thee interchanged with darknes, which thou mightst as easily
have commanded to be perpetuall', and concluded that 'the
continuance of the best things, cloieth and wearieth: there is
nothing but thy self, wherein there is not satiety', so that 'the
vicitude of things' pleases most, and 'the inter-course even of
those occurrents which in their owne nature are lesse worthy,
gives more contentment, then the unaltered estate of better'.[3]
The plenitude of the universe was recognized by these two
writers, its mystery and its change; but though change was
inevitable, it was not regarded pessimistically. There was an
ambiguity about the attitude to temporality during this period
which held grief and optimism in conjunction. During the
sixteenth century, and still commonly in the seventeenth, the
mournful note prevailed, the lamentation over the ravages of
time, especially among humankind, issuing in many poems

[1] Adolphe Coster, 'Baltasar Graçian', *Revue hispanique*, xxiv (1913), relates this
theme to a twelfth-century Arabic romance by Hagy ben Yaqzan, which was known
to Albertus Magnus and translated into Hebrew and Latin.
[2] *El Criticon*, chap. iii.
[3] *Works* (1647), p. 772: 'The Creation'.

whose framework was a comparison between man and the creatures. Yet in time the natural order continued, the creatures fulfilled their pattern, in contrast to man, who caused the only deviations. So the very contemplation of change might teach man his duty; for the temporal both hid and revealed the eternal.[1] There was a good kind of alteration, a legitimate magic, as well as the evil change which ended in destruction. 'What makes the chain of admiration is novelty, both in Nature and in Art.'[2]

Both Hall and Gracián share another attitude: the nature of the universe is ultimately enigmatic, in its concealment of God, in 'the appearance of disorder' which is 'a riddle of Providence',[3] and towards which wonder is the most appropriate gesture.

Hear me, said *Andrenio*, this last truth the greatest, and most sublime of any, that I have yet declared. I confess, that though I have admired four strange Prodigies in this Universe, *viz.* The multitude and variety of Creatures, the harmony and agreement in Contraries, their beauty and ornament mixed with profit, and convenience, and their mutations with Permanency. Yet above all, I remained confused in the knowledge of the Creator, who is so manifest in his Creatures, and yet hid in himself; whose Attributes are imprinted on every step, and action of his Work. . . And notwithstanding this great God is hid, though known, not seen, though manifest, far distant, though near; this is that riddle which hath confused my Understanding, and left me in an extasie of love, and adoration.[4]

When Robert Boyle the scientist had his 'Discourse Touching Occasional Meditations' published as a preface to his *Occasional Reflections upon Several Subjects* (1665), his interest in meditative practice was already somewhat *démodé*. Though he was conscious of Hall's example, he also expressed some surprise that he had not discussed the utility of meditation, but had assumed it. Boyle himself, in undertaking to repair this

---

[1] See *Faerie Queene*, VII. vii. 58.
[2] Gracián, *El Criticon*, chap. iii. Cf. Hall, *Occasional Meditations*, v, 'Upon a faire Prospect'; and see C. DeWitt Thorpe, 'Addison and Some of his Predecessors on "Novelty" ', *Publications of the Modern Language Association of America*, lii (1937), 1114–29.
[3] Rycaut, *The Critick*, p. 21.   [4] Ibid., pp. 38–39.

omission, showed an uneasiness about the acceptability of his subject: he had to prove to his public that meditation was not only good but useful, and that pious and profane alike would find some value in it, a strengthening of wit as well as of will and affections. He himself was apparently unable to recognize something hardly innocent about his way of recommending 'this innocent kind of necromancy', as he called occasional meditation, by pleading worldly expediency and self-love as the next best motives to genuine devotion. He had already detected the general temper which would provoke Shadwell and Swift and Shaftesbury to parody and criticize this form of writing.[1] He expected to be accused of a 'very neglected' and 'luxuriant strain', of triviality in his choice of subject, of forced analogies and the over-stretching of parallels, of redundant descriptions, of a style 'disproportionate to such mean and trifling subjects'. By being on the defensive, he brought into sharp focus some of the impulses implicit in the literary habits of the earlier seventeenth century, and particularly the relation between piety and wit. Meditation, he wrote, satisfies man's thirst for variety. 'Variety is a thing so pleasing to humane Nature, that there are many things, which it, either alone, or chiefly, recommends to us.' The capacity of the imagination is infinite, and so is satisfied with no less than the scope of the universe, which is available to 'be so many ways consider'd, and so variously compounded'. Even the practised contemplator is frequently surprised by finding unexpected likenesses between the most distant and unrelated objects. 'For one of the chief accounts, upon which Wit it self is delightful, is . . . the unexpectedness of the things that please us; that unexpectedness being the highest Degree of Novelty.' It is also better because more dexterous to find one's own emblems rather than to depend on books. 'And so, from Ethical or Theological Composures, to take out Lessons that may improve the Mind, is a thing much inferiour to the being able to do the like out of the Book of Nature, where most Matters that are not Physical, if

---

[1] Shadwell, *The Virtuoso* (1676); Swift, 'Meditation upon a Broomstick'; Shaftesbury, *Characteristicks* (1711).

they seem not to be purposely veil'd, are at least but darkly hinted'.[1] Nor need the meditator keep strictly to his subject: his mind should be let as loose as a greyhound after its quarry, to range over secular and sacred matters alike. Such contemplation also improves the intelligence, making men more observant to notice the qualities of things, to recognize spiritual significance in the least likely subjects, to have a ready and original wit, a pliant, neat, and inventive style, and skill in making comparisons, 'strange and unobvious'.[2] The contemplator would thus, he promised, become both 'devout and ingenious'.[3]

By the end of the seventeenth century, the limitations of this sort of meditative practice seemed to be as apparent as its virtues.

The Manner of Exercise is call'd *Meditation*, and is of a sort so solemn and profound, that we dare not so much as thorowly examine the Subject on which we are bid to meditate.[4]

Instead of looking narrowly into his own Nature and Mind, that he may be no longer a Mystery to himself, he is taken up with the Contemplation of other mysterious Natures, which he can never explain or comprehend.[5]

It is possible to detect here the irritation of good breeding at a wonder which can express itself only by departing from the civilized orders of language in the direction of 'enigmatical Wit'. Parables and double meanings are an illicit deception; the recognition of mystery is an excuse for a lack of straightforward thinking. The magic of words which 'varies all shapes, and mixes all extremes' is no longer acceptable.[6] Wonder and understanding are set in opposition; and the harmony of the universe is offered as a model for literary orderliness. 'Now the Works of God, tho infinitely various, are extremely regular.'[7]

---

[1] *Occasional Reflections*, pp. 13–18.   [2] Ibid., pp. 39–42.
[3] Ibid., p. 75.
[4] *Characteristicks* (5th ed., Birmingham, 1773), i. 343, 'Advice to an Author'.
[5] Ibid., p. 175.
[6] Ibid., pp. 63, 120, 175, and Addison, *Spectator*, lxiii.
[7] John Dennis, *Critical Works*, ed. E. N. Hooker (Baltimore 1939–43), i. 335, 'The Grounds of Criticism in Poetry'.

The sense of mystifying plenitude was giving way to a sense
of division and limitation, to the decorum of one thing at a
time.[1] The small had no longer equal value with the great; and
the idea that ugliness might be beautiful from another point of
view was a kind of blasphemy. Men could no longer wonder
at what was beneath them; but wonder was reserved for what
was elevated, not for the minute, the commonplace, or the
eccentric.[2] The language of riddle and paradox, of the harmony
of discords, had been superseded.

II

Enumeration, the simplest and often the dullest way of expressing admiration for the universe, was given justification not only
by classical precedent but also from the nature-psalms, which
were frequently paraphrased during our period.[3] The simple
scheme of *benedicite, omnia opera* was a favoured one, yet the
creatures might perform other offices besides the uncom-
plicated offering of praise. They might illustrate divine providence, or they might belittle human efforts and excellences.
Or the plenitude of the natural world might hide God from
man rather than revealing Him. The movement of search and
finding is the pattern of such poems as Herbert's 'Peace' and
'The Search', in which the poet asks one creature after another
where God is to be found. Such colloquies with the creatures
were made familiar in meditative practice;[4] lying behind them
is the knowledge of Biblical conversations between man and
beast, such as Job xii, and the search of the lover for the
beloved in *Canticles*. St. Augustine had made his own quest
among the creatures, which he recorded in the *Confessions*, x:

I put the Question (*saith he*) to the Earth, and to the Sea; and to

[1] See G. Williamson, 'The Rhetorical Pattern of Neo-Classical Wit', *Modern Philo-
ogy*, xxxiii (1935–6), 55–81.
[2] Dennis, ibid. i. 227, 353, 340.
[3] Examples are Psalm civ by Sidney, Bacon, Abraham Fraunce, James II, Sir Edwin
Sandys, Carew, and Henry Vaughan; Psalm cxlviii by Thomas Stanley and the Earl
of Roscommon.
[4] See Martz, *The Poetry of Meditation*, p. 37.

the rest of the Creatures; and they give me an Answer; Now if you
would know what my Question was; It was the deep intention,
and consideration, I had in my heart, about the Creatures; And
would you know what their Answer was; their Answer was what
I had collected in my Meditations, from their several Natures,
qualities, and properties.[1]

But the seeker in Herbert's poems does not find so simply;
there is a human frustration about his first inquiries which
makes the inner resolution of the conclusion more telling.
'Peace'[2] has the concrete qualities of a child's tale: though he
has sought amongst the creatures for peace, all they have
showed him is impermanence, 'A hollow winde' in 'a secret
cave', the clouds about the rainbow which 'immediately / Did
break and scatter', the 'Crown Imperiall' in the garden which
had a worm at its root. At length 'a rev'rend good old man'
told him of the 'Prince of old' who 'At Salem dwelt', and from
whose grave grew 'twelve stalks of wheat: / Which many
wondring at, got some of those / To plant and set.'

> Take of this grain, which in my garden grows,
>   And grows for you;
> Make bread of it: and that repose
>   And peace, which ev'ry where
> With so much earnestnesse you do pursue,
>   Is onely there.

'The Search'[3] is a less parabolic, more direct address to 'My
Lord, my Love', a pleading argument for God's return to his
experience. Both 'the sphere And centre' deny God's presence,
he has sent out sighs which return without discovery; yet it
seems as though some of the creatures already know what he
still seeks.

---

[1] Quoted by Ralph Austen, *A Dialogue betweene the Husbandman, and Fruit-trees*
(Oxford, 1676), sig. A^r, alongside Aquinas, sig. A2^v: 'When we *seriously consider, the
nature, and properties* of inanimate creatures; then we *aske Questions* of them; and they
being thus Questioned, they return an *answer* unto men, when we clearly perceive
that their wonderfull *Natures, vertues, and properties*, cannot be, but from the *Power,
and Wisdome of a superior Cause*.'
[2] *Works*, ed. F. E. Hutchinson (Clarendon Press, Oxford, 1941), p. 124.
[3] Ibid., pp. 162–3.

Yet can I mark how herbs below
　　Grow green and gay,
As if to meet thee they did know,
　　While I decay.
Yet can I mark how starres above
　　Simper and shine,
As having keyes unto thy love,
　　While poor I pine.

The search was a theme which belonged to secular pastoral poetry.[1] Among religious poets Casimir Sarbiewski had a poem of this kind, and in England William Habington, Thomas Heywood, and Thomas Beedome.[2] Henry Vaughan's poems 'The Dwelling-place', 'The Search', and 'Vanity of Spirit' were written according to this pattern, the first and second with the human Christ as the object of their quest.

　　What happy, secret fountain,
　　Fair shade, or mountain,
Whose undiscover'd virgin glory
Boasts it this day, though not in story,
Was then thy dwelling? did some cloud
Fix'd to a Tent, descend and shroud
My distrest Lord? or did a star
Becken'd by thee, though high and far,
In sparkling smiles haste gladly down
To lodge light, and increase her own?
My dear, dear God! I do not know
What lodgd thee then, nor where, nor how;
But I am sure, thou dost now come
Oft to a narrow, homely room,
Where thou too hast but the least part,
My God, I mean *my sinful heart*.[3]

[1] See William Browne, 'A Sigh from Oxford', and *Britannia's Pastorals* (1613, 1616), I. iv. 395 ff. (the search of Aletheia), II. ii. 493 ff. (the search for Mira); Michael Drayton, 'The Quest of Cynthia'; William Cartwright, 'A Sigh'.

[2] Matthias-Casimir Sarbiewski, *Lyricorum Libri tres* (Cologne, 1625), II. ix. translated by G. Hill, *The Odes of Casimire* (1646), 31; William Habington, *Castara*, 1640, 'Dominum dominantium'; Thomas Heywood, *The Hierarchie*, pp. 53–56, A Meditation on the first Tractate, pp. 108–9, A Meditation on the second Tractate, pp. 619–22, A Meditation on the ninth Tractate; Thomas Beedome, *Poems Divine, and Humane* (1641), 'The Inquisition'.

[3] *Works*, ed. L. C. Martin (2nd ed., Clarendon Press, Oxford, 1958), p. 516.

'The Search' and 'Vanity of Spirit' are both informed with a sense of the limitations to the knowledge of God acquired through the creatures, which are at once the cause of delight and yet secretive, imperfect messengers because of man's evil choices ('The Search' has 'The skinne, and shell of things', 'Vanity of Spirit' has 'Hyerogliphicks quite dismembred'),[1] any clear answers being reserved for heaven, or for a momentary insight upon earth.

So the contemplation of variety might have an effect other than comprehension; it might conclude in that worship whose best language is one of negatives. To argue *ex visibilibus invisibilia* was a common procedure.

. . . nay the beauties of Gods creatures cannot be considered of without wonder, without astonishment. If then such be the visible things of nature, what shall wee thinke the invisible are?[2]

Rhetorically speaking, this was the procedure of the figure called 'Progression', 'Which by steps of comparison scores every degree till it comes to the top'.[3]

> And, as the Suns light, in streames n'ere so faire
> Is but a shadow, to his light in aire,
> His splendor that in aire we so admire,
> Is but a shadow to his beames in fire:
> In fire his brightnesse, but a shadow is
> To radiance fir'd, in that pure brest of his:[4]

So while a sense of nature's plenitude might issue in the simplest kind of poetry, it might at the other extreme become an awareness of the enigmatic quality of the universe which could be expressed only in an appropriately complicated style.

Aenigma is properly *obscura allegoria*, an allegory with a mask on; it is a borrowed speech and a cloudy speech. A knotty intricate speech sealed up and lockt from vulgar apprehensions; that's a

1 *Works* (1958), pp. 407, 419.
2 Thomaso Buoni, *Problemes of Beautie*, translated Samson Lennard (n.d., but dedication dated 1606), sig. B9ᵛ. Cf. Rom. i. 20.
3 John Hoskyns, *Directions for Speech and Style* (written *c.* 1599–1600, ed. Hoyt W. Hudson, Princeton, 1935), p. 26.
4 George Chapman, *Poems*, ed. P. B. Bartlett (New York, 1941), p. 225, 'A Hymne to our Saviour on the Crosse'.

riddle: and our knowledge of God here is thus cloudy and enigmatical. . . . The world is, as one calls it, *Aenigma Dei*.[1]

Nathanael Culverwell had the two-way look towards devotion
and rhetoric shared by his contemporaries, as his rendering of
his text, 1 Cor. xiii. 12 suggests: 'We see through a glasse
darkely in a riddle.'[2] It is significant that he turned to Bacon
for support of his view:

This way of beholding him breeds rather admiration then begets
knowledge; for when we hear of so goodly an Essence that hath all
excellencies bound up in one vast volume, we wonder what that
should be: and admiration is at the best but *semen scientiae*, or *abrupta
scientia*, as the learned *Verulam* calls it, a *stupified kinde of knowledge*.[3]

The world expresses God as the words of an enigma express
their hidden subject, 'by superlatives', that is, by its variety of
glories which although heaped together only hide the mystery
of the Godhead,[4] by presenting effects from which a cause may
be inferred,[5] by negatives from which the concealed reality
may be guessed at, and by paradox.[6] To meditate upon the
creatures is at once to be aware of the divine and to be impeded
by materiality; and the consequence is longing rather than
satisfaction.

It is no accident that the image of the robe appeared frequently
amongst the most familiar ways both of conveying a sense of
the world's mystery and plenitude and of describing the procedure of literary myths and fictions. It was quite as natural for
the Renaissance poet to express his sense of cosmic abundance
through the description of a symbolic figure as through the
description of landscape; and frequently this figure was given

---

[1] N. Culverwell, *Spiritual Opticks* (1651), in *An Elegant and Learned Discourse of the
Light of Nature with several other Treatises* (1652), pp. 181, 187.

[2] The Vulgate has *per speculum in aenigmate videre*.

[3] Ed. cit., p. 182. Cf. *The Advancement of Learning*, ed. cit. ii, fol. 114.

[4] Ed. cit., p. 182: 'Many divine perfections are scattered and broken amongst the
creatures, as the same face may be represented in several Glasses; and all the excellencies
of the creatures are collected, and meet eminently in God.'

[5] See Sir Thomas Browne, *Enquiries into Vulgar and Common Errors*, I. iii, on the
superiority of this to other uses of the creatures.

[6] Cf. Culverwell's example from Dionysius the Areopagite, 'the transcendent
beams of Divine darknesse' and Vaughan, 'The Night'.

a representative garment. The elaborate robe or veil expressive of the character or function of its wearer is one of the favourite descriptive subjects in epic and romance literature. Sidney's *Arcadia* contains many such descriptions which, whatever their relationship to contemporary fashion, had a definite ritual importance, standing in more ways than one for human lordship over the universe. One of these garments was made of watered material, 'at each side whereof he had nettings cast over, in which were divers fishes naturally made, & so pretily, that as the horse stirred, the fishes seemed to strive, and leape in the nette'.[1] A coat of armour, with its furniture, 'seemed a pleasant garden, wherein grewe orange trees, which with their golden fruites, cunningly beaten in, & embrodered, greatly enriched the eye-pleasing colour of greene'.[2] There were of course classical precedents for this habit, such as the embroidery in Claudian's *De raptu Proserpinae*, the skirt of Diana, 'On whose light ground (unmatched to behold), / The wandring *Delos* floats in seas of gold', and Proserpine's own dress, representing the birth of the sun and the moon.[3]

During our period, the Lady Nature appears with several names and under several guises.[4] In Drayton's *Endimion and Phoebe* (1595), in his *The Man in the Moone* (1606), and in John Hagthorpe's *Visiones Rerum* (1623)[5] she is present with different parts of her garb representing earth, air, and sea; in Giles Fletcher's poem *Christs Victorie and Triumph* (1610) she is Mercy who upholds the world, wearing a garment woven by her own hand, 'With threads, so fresh and lively coloured, / That seem'd the world she newe created thear'.[6] All the universe wonders at Lady Nature, as a lover admires his beloved. And her mystery, besides her palpable beauty, might be suggested by her robes. For the details of Nature's appearance

[1] *Arcadia* (1590), ed. A. E. Feuillerat (Cambridge, 1912), p. 105.
[2] Ibid., p. 462.
[3] i. 246–68; ii. 34–35, 41–54. Translation by Leonard Digges (1617), sig. E3ʳ.
[4] E. C. Knowlton, 'The Goddess Nature in Early Periods', *Journal of English and Germanic Philology*, xix (1920), 224–53; 'Nature in Middle English', ibid. xx (1921), 186–207.
[5] 'Cursus et Ordo Rerum.'
[6] 'Christs Victorie in Heaven', liii.

Spenser was pleased to refer to 'Dan Geffrey', except for 'a veile that wimpled every where', hiding her head and face, 'that mote to non appeare',[1] and thus concealing both her terror and her beauty, which human beings dared not look upon. She is not Nature in its materiality, but in its first principles, akin to Wisdom of the *Proverbs*, who sits at God's feet and dispenses His laws. Associated with this personage is Uranore of Henry More's 'Psychozoia' (1642), who represents divine activity immanent in the universe, and whose fourfold wedding-garment is described in paradoxes. 'Her stole aethereall . . . though so high it be, down to the earth doth fall';[2] it is a 'myst'ry rare' that 'thickned veile should maken things appear more bare'.[3]

The robe, too, might convey the idea of the imaginative concealment of truth for the further illumination of it. Sometimes it was the quality of accommodation of higher truths to a simpler level which received emphasis.

> Weake eyes that cannot (like the Eagle) brooke
> The brightnes of the Sun, through Lawne must looke.[4]

Sometimes it was the riddling quality of fictitious writing which was stressed. The ancient myths 'as by veils invented with ingenuity . . . have hidden all the secrets of Nature and Philosophy'.[5] The *Metamorphoses* of Ovid are like the silken scarves worn publicly by Persian monarchs to induce respect.[6]

> So Truth lay under Fables, that the Eye
> Might Reverence the Mystery, not descry. . .
> Thus is your Dress so Order'd, so Contriv'd,
> As 'tis but only Poetry Reviv'd.[7]

The idea that the true character of things can on occasion be represented only by using the language of paradox whose crux

[1] *Faerie Queene*, VII. vii. 5.   [2] Ibid. I. xxix, xxxix.
[3] Ibid. xxvii.
[4] William Basse, *Urania: The Woman in the Moone*, in *The Poetical Works*, ed. R. W. Bond (1893), p. 314.
[5] The preface to Ripa, *Iconologia* (Rome, 1593).
[6] The preface to Arthur Golding, *The XV Bookes of P. Ovidius Naso, entytuled Metamorphosis* (1565-7), sig. Aii^v.
[7] William Cartwright, 'On a Gentlewomans Silk-hood' in *Plays and Poems*, ed. G. Blakemore Evans (Madison-Wisconsin, 1951), pp. 483-4.

is the harmony of discords is an ancient one. To the later sixteenth century anything which contradicted common opinion
might be called paradoxical: Du Bartas described the Coper-
nican theory in this way.[1] But Aristotle had defined the circle
paradoxically in a stricter sense: 'it is a very great marvel that
contraries should be present together, and the circle is made up
of contraries',[2] motion and rest, the concave and the convex,
the ability to move both backwards and forwards at once.
'These are as much opposed to one another', he wrote, 'as the
great is to the small.' The contemplation of the union of such
opposites as soul and body, not only in man, but 'in the least
flye that is'[3] provoked a not dissimilar sense of wonder in
Augustine at 'this stupendious combination'. This was indeed
believed to be the principle which bound together the universe,
the *discordia concors* which tamed the opposing elements.

In 1594 there appeared in English a treatise, rendered from
the French of Louis Le Roy, called *Of the Interchangeable Course
or Variety of Things in the Whole World*,[4] which dealt at large
with this idea that the world is 'maintayned by contraries'. Its
interest lies partly in the style which results from the consideration of variety, whose devices range from the use of
enumeration and balanced phrases to contrast and paradox.

It is not then without cause, that nature is so desirous of contraries,
making of them, all decency, and beautie; not of things which are
of like nature. This kind of tempering is the cause, that such things
as before were divers and different, do accord and agree together,
to establish, intertain, and embellish one an other, the contrarietie,
becomming unitie; and the discord concord; the enmitie amitie;
and contention covenant.[5]

In 1600 appeared a poem composed by John Norden the topo-
grapher, *Vicissitudo Rerum*, reprinted in 1601 as *A Store-House of
Varieties, Briefly discoursing the Change and Alteration of things in*

[1] See Sylvester, ed. cit., p. 76.   [2] *Mechanica*, 847[b]18–19.
[3] *St. Augustine, of The Citie of God* (1610), translated by John Healey, XXII.
XXIV. 907.
[4] *De la Vicissitude ou Variété des choses en l'univers* (1577), translated by Richard
Ashley, 1594.
[5] Ibid., fol. 5[v].

this world,[1] which on scrutiny appears to be firmly based on the prose treatise, and to show even more stylistic effects of the same kind. Changes in the universe, wrote Norden, 'proceede of contraries, / That in them breede such strange varieties'.[2] So one element may change into another, because contrary qualities are inherent in them. He was fascinated by the 'strange diversities' of things, and invented several paradoxical phrases, on the model of Lucan's *concordia discors*,[3] to express briefly the harmony of disparates: 'concording *enmitie*', 'discording *union*', and 'concording *discord*'.[4] Norden recognized the union of opposites as a principle operating in all the arts: 'All *Arts* have *discord*, yet in unitie Concording.'

> Some *contraries* accord, some disagree.
> Yet perfit is Dame *Natures* art in things:
> For by dissent, she true *assenting* brings.[5]

Il Cannocchiale Aristotelico (Turin, 1654) by Emmanuelo Tesauro is one of the most unmistakably clear expositions from the seventeenth century of the idea that the best kind of poetry is enigmatic; and it is no coincidence that this should be associated with wonder at the world's surprises. The most noble part of wit is the marvellous, '*il Mirabile*', and the very heart of the marvellous is '*l'Enigma*', which is a witty speech, composed of two disparate terms.[6] 'And those will be more delightful in which appear three characteristics: that is, unity in diversity, clarity in obscurity, and deception in anticipation.'[7] The riddle is part of the seventh kind of metaphor, '*di Opposizione*',[8] which is the most spirited of all kinds of wit. The wit of contraries may consist of verbal harmony alone, of balanced and patterned syntax, or it may be a harmony of two incompatible and astonishing ideas. It may be frivolous, or it may be

---

[1] See Kathrine Kroller, 'Two Elizabethan Expressions of the Idea of Mutability', *Studies in Philology*, xxxv (1938), 228–37.

[2] St. 46.

[3] Lucan, *Pharsalia*, i. 98.

[4] Sts. 84, 90, 94.

[5] Sts. 96, 98.

[6] Op. cit., p. 550. He refers to Aristotle, *Ars Poetica*, xxi.

[7] 'Et quegli saran più dilettevoli, ne' quali appaiono tre proprietà: cioè; *Unità nella diversità: Chiarezza nella oscurità: Inganno nella espettatione.*'

[8] Ibid., pp. 531 ff.

elevated.[1] It may consist of only two words, or of sentences; it may be a proverb, a witty reply, or a description.[2] It gravitates towards oxymoron and paradox.

Now all this was not really new: poetic licence in the use of extreme figures such as *metalepsis, catachresis, allegoria,* and *aenigma* had already received theoretical justification.[3] What is original is the grouping of kinds of figure to lead up to the riddle as their climax.

For the fabrication of riddles in Renaissance Europe, the important events were the publication in 1533 of the *Aenigmata* of Symposius, in 1551 of the *Aenigmata* of Gyraldus, an anthology of ancient definitions and examples, and in 1596 of the *Aenigmatographia* of Reusner, which included the whole of Gyraldus.[4] Reusner's work was a convenient collection for a cultivated public of the main body of classical and Renaissance theory, accompanied by the riddles of Symposius, of Aldhelm, and of several major sixteenth-century Latinists. The riddle, like the emblem, was an appropriate expression of a society hankering after the esoteric, an *élite* of the initiated possessing some sort of special knowledge not shared by the crowd; and they might both be used either frivolously or seriously without indecorum.

There is considerable evidence to suggest that the cult of emblem-making was closely associated with the popularity of riddles. Henri Estienne is typical among the theorists of the emblem in distinguishing, in *The Art of Making Devises,* between two kinds of figure and of image, one clear and the other obscure, each existing in its own right. For the genuine

[1] Tesauro, pp. 535, 550.   [2] Op. cit., pp. 545-50.

[3] See Rosemund Tuve, *Elizabethan and Metaphysical Imagery* (Chicago, 1947), pp. 130-8; Henry Peacham the Elder, *The Garden of Eloquence* (1577); George Puttenham, *The Arte of English Poesie* (1589), III. vii; Charles Butler, *Rhetoricae Libri Duo* (1629), sig. B^r, based on Petrus Ramus, *Rhetorica* (ed. of Hanover, 1608, p. 8).

[4] J. C. Wernsdorf, *Poetae Latini Minores* (Helmstadt, 1794), vi, has both text and bibliography of Symposius, *Aenigmata.* His riddles were reprinted in Nicholas Caussin, *De Symbolica Aegyptiorum Sapientia* (Paris, 1618), side by side with the emblems of Horapollo and the *Physiologus.* A second edition of Reusner (Frankfurt, 1602) contained the riddles of Aldhelm, which had appeared in 1601 in the edition of R. P. Martinus Delrio. J. C. Castalio had his anthology of riddles (*Aenigmata et griphi veterum ac recentium*), published in 1604.

emblem 'may demonstrate things universall, and hold the rank of morall precepts, which may as wel serve for all the world as for the proper author of the *Emblem*', whereas the device is applicable to the case of one person alone, 'veyled . . . under a knotty conceit of words and figures', and used particularly to convey private feelings.[1] Similitudes might be 'common and triviall', or they might contain 'holy and mysticall doctrine'.[2] For his conception of *aenigma*, which was technically separate from both emblem and device, Estienne followed the classical authorities commonly respected by Renaissance writers on the subject, Clearchus and Athenaeus, Aulus Gellius, Diomedes, Donatus and Fabius.[3] 'The Aenigma . . . is an obscure sentence, expressed by an occult similitude of things, or it is a speech hard to be understood in respect of the obscurity of the Allegory.' So ran the frequently quoted definition of Diomedes. Clearchus described it as 'a sportive question, which exacts an information of the matter, contained in the sentence proposed, be it for honour or reprehension'; but he also allowed it 'in serious matters, and in other subjects of Philosophie'.[4]

Tesauro distinguished four different kinds of *mirabili*: the marvels of nature, of art, of opinion, and of deception, and his examples, in subject and style alike, are commonplaces of his period. Indeed, his vernacular source-book might have been Du Bartas's *Deux Semaines*, the poem whose style has been lately described as a derivative of St. Basil's in his *Hexaemeron*.[5] And Erasmus, in a preface to his works, had praised Basil for his wit and his riddles.[6] Du Bartas, with his distinct preference for curiosities, and for pointing out the oddity of the common-place, did for many creatures what the writers of the *Greek Anthology* had done for birds, beasts, and insects, what Claudian had done in his familiar short poems for the porcupine, for Archimedes' sphere, for the burning-glass, what Symposius

[1] Op. cit., p. 10.   [2] Ibid., pp. 4–8.
[3] Gyraldus summarized Diomedes, Donatus, Fabius, Athenaeus (*Deipnosophistae*, x. 457). Reusner included Aulus Gellius (*Noctes Atticae*, xii. 6 and xviii. 2).
[4] Estienne, op. cit., p. 6.
[5] M. Thibaut de Maisières, *Les Poèmes inspirés du Début de la Genèse à l'Époque de la Renaissance* (Louvain, 1931), p. 40.
[6] Basilius Magnus, *Opera* (Basle, 1532).

and other minor riddlers in Latin had also attempted: he turned them into marvels.

The first mystery of existence is the Godhead, the second His creatures the monsters, which are *argutezze della natura*, nature's witty jokes. Tesauro's examples are of creatures which belong to two elements: the satyr, the minotaur, sea-oxen, the phoenix, the silkworm, the tortoise. Farther down the scale of nature come the inanimate creatures, the river Meander which moves and yet does not, Claudian's Mount Aetna, where ice and fire live side by side.[1] Earthquakes, storms, lightning, comets, meteors—all these are enigmatic and marvellous.

The wonders of art include the ship, the clock, and Architas' dove (described by Du Bartas).[2] The wonders of opinion are illusions of different kinds, both to the eye and to the intelligence, such as the reversal of movement and stillness from the vantage-point of a vehicle (Virgil's *litora diffugiunt* for *navis fugit*), reflections in the water (*Aequor et in Coelo videas, et in Aequore Coelum*), pictures which though artifacts seem real, and theatrical machinery, the subject of an epigram by Martial. Here the language of paradox is necessary to convey the deception of the senses; and the mistakes of the imagination are allied to the ingenuities of art.

In the section called 'Mirabili di Fingimento' the emphasis is more conspicuously on stylistic manipulations of the plain world to convey a sense of wonder, or even to idealize the mean and joke about the elevated. This may be done either lengthily,[3] in the allegorical metaphor (the examples are two riddling periphrases for the year), in a succession of unrelated conceits applying to one theme (an example is *Vidi carnem humanam, Ossibus ludentem, in Campo ligneo*), in sustained periphrastic description (such as Claudian's *Phoenix*), or briefly,

---

[1] See also Puttenham, op. cit., III. xviii, and Sylvester, ed. cit., p. 24: a riddle of ice and water; Peacham, *The Garden of Eloquence* (2nd ed., 1593), p. 28, under *Aenigma*: a tree-riddle.

[2] Sylvester, ed. cit., pp. 133–4.

[3] Pp. 542 ff. Puttenham defined *periphrasis* as a figure which hides by describing something more lengthily than is necessary.

in different kinds of equivocal or paradoxical statement. Amongst these Tesauro discussed the 'Diffinition Mirabile Enigmatica', 'confined within two incompatible terms, one of which conveys the likeness, and the other the difference',[1] that is, at its purest, oxymoron. The equivocal definition names something metaphorically and then sets limitations to the name, which may even be a negation of it. So the echo is *anima inanima*, the bat is *avem non avem*, the dogstar is a dog which neither steals, eats, nor sleeps, the celestial arc is a bow without a string. Du Bartas has his examples of this type of definition: the dolphin is 'the stern-less Boat, and bit-less Horse'.[2] Other common word-patterns for describing the creatures which Tesauro recognized were the combination of positive with positive (his examples are periphrases for the echo: speaking stone, living rock, daughter of the breath, and so on), and of negative with negative (the echo is neither man nor beast, it neither speaks nor keeps silent). The nature of a creature might also be defined in a proposition rather than a short phrase: the silkworm makes its nest its tomb, it dies a worm and rises a winged creature. Or a whole poem might be built up by finding as many analogies as possible between two disparates, such as a queen and a rose, and gathering these likenesses up in witty phrases; or by making as many variations as possible on one theme, such as the bee in amber.[3] This sort of poem is discussed in the section describing the Metaphor of Deception, and in company with 'the playful praise of animals and mean creatures'.

The English poets seem to have been on the whole attracted towards the making of straight circumlocutions, towards the many-in-one type of riddle popular with Du Bartas, or towards the kind of oxymoron in which the negative is only implied. Donne was not averse to the most curious and grotesque periphrases for things, the creatures included, especially in *The Progress of the Soule*. Particular interest, however, attaches itself

---

[1] 'Ristretta in due Termini incompatibili: l'un de' quali sia come il Genere; l'altro la Differenza.'
[2] Ed. cit., p. 102.
[3] Tesauro, op. cit., pp. 539, 577.

to the frequency of oxymoron and paradox in the prose of
Arcadia. Sidney's own attitude is probably reflected in John
Hoskyns's remarks about the use of extreme figures in his
Directions for Speech and Style:

> Sometimes it expresseth a thing in the highest degree of possibility,
> beyond the truth, that it descending thence may find the truth;
> sometimes in flat impossibility, that rather you may conceive the
> unspeakableness than the untruth of the relation.[1]

The figure which we know as oxymoron was called rather
Synœciosis during our period.[2] Sometimes the term is applied
to a longer statement which we would call paradox.[3] The elder
Peacham allowed it only in satire. But most probably because
of its frequent appearance in *Arcadia*, the term was given a
rehabilitation by Hoskyns, who applied it to either oxymoron
or paradox. The words which he used to describe the figure are
consonant with the contemporary outlook: truth is sometimes
so strange as to be expressible only in a harmony of opposites.

> Synœciosis is a composition of contraries, and by both words
> intimateth the meaning of neither precisely but a moderation and
> mediocrity of both. . . . This is a fine course to stir admiration in
> the hearer, and make them think it a strange harmony which must
> be expressed in such discords; therefore this example shall conclude:
>
> > There was so perfect agreement in so mortal disagreement,
> > like a music made of cunning discords.
>
> This is an easy figure now in fashion, not like ever to be so usual.[4]

Among nature's riddles, providence was regarded as one of
the strangest during our period: 'in *the wayes of Providence*,
those designes that in respect of our apprehensions are carried
on by a crypticall involved method, are yet in themselves of
as excellent contrivance, as any of those, that seem to be of
more facile and perspicuous order.'[5] It is therefore not surprising

---

[1] Ed. cit., p. 29.

[2] See Quintilian, *Institutio Oratoria*, IX. iii. 64; Peacham, *The Garden of Eloquence*,
2nd ed. (1593), pp. 170–1.

[3] Puttenham, *The Arte of English Poesie*, III. xix.   [4] Op. cit., pp. 36–37.

[5] John Wilkins, *The Beauty of Providence*, p. 69. Cf. Bacon, *The Advancement of
Learning*, ed. cit., book ii, fol. 16ᵛ, and Culverwell, *Spirituall Opticks*, ed. cit., p. 189

to find Herbert, in one of his less distinguished yet interesting poems on the creatures, called 'Providence', adopting a deliberately paradoxical style. On the one hand he was as aware as any of his generation that God's will is mysterious, reversing common expectations ('Tempests are calm to thee; they know thy hand, / And hold it fast, as children do their fathers, / Which crie and follow'; 'E'vn poysons praise thee'), that the creatures instruct and warn man in odd ways ('Birds teach us hawking; fishes have their net:', 'Thou hast hid metals: man may take them thence; / But at his perill: when he digs the place, / He makes a grave'), that nature's apparent dangers and limitations are often good ('The sea, which seems to stop the traveller, / Is by a ship the speedier passage made'), that the world's plenitude is unfailingly astonishing ('Thou art in small things great, not small in any', 'And if an herb hath power, what have the starres? / A rose, besides his beautie, is a cure'). Yet he is sufficiently convinced of ultimate order to use a patterned and balanced language sometimes euphuistic, sometimes Bartasian, sometimes almost Augustan. And the superfluities of Sylvester's Du Bartas are curbed by his epigrammatic use of the four-line stanza. Du Bartas's favourite method of constructing a riddle was to show how many contradictory properties were united in one subject, after the manner of Claudian's *fert omnia secum*. Herbert composed his own imitation concerning 'The Indian nut alone', which 'Is clothing, meat and trencher, drink and can, / Boat, cable, sail and needle, all in one.' Another complete stanza is built up as a series of riddles such as Tesauro admired, only supplying their own answers.

> Light without winde is glasse: warm without weight
> Is wooll and furre: cool without closenesse, shade:
> Speed without pains, a horse: tall without height,
> A servile hawk: low without losse, a spade.

In his *Novum Organum* Bacon had a discussion of 'Singular Instances', those phenomena, such as the magnet, quicksilver, and the elephant, which still seemed miraculous because the

laws which governed their nature had not yet been found, and
of their relatives, 'Bordering Instances', that is, phenomena
'which appear to be composed of two species', 'Moss, which
is something between Putrescence and a Plant; . . . Comets,
which hold a place between Stars and ignited Meteors; . . .
flying Fishes, between Fishes and Birds; . . . Bats, between
Birds and Quadrupeds.'[1] These were the creatures between
two conditions which had particularly interested Aristotle in
his serious biological investigations, besides being matter for
diversion.[2] It was with 'Bordering Instances', those singularities
which were the appropriate subjects, according to contemporary theory,[3] for an epigrammatic style, that Herbert concluded his celebration of signs of providence among the
creatures.

> Frogs marry fish and flesh; bats, bird and beast;
> Sponges, non-sense and sense; mines, th'earth & plants.
>
> To show thou art not bound, as if thy lot
> Were worse then ours, sometimes thou shiftest hands.
> Most things move th'under-jaw; the Crocodile not.
> Most things sleep lying; th'Elephant leans or stands.[4]

The modern reader may consider that such lines reduce the
mystery of the universe in an attempt to express it, but for
Herbert the creatures were at once worthy of awe and of

---

[1] *Novum Organum* II. xxviii, xxx.

[2] See A. O. Lovejoy, *The Great Chain of Being* (Harvard, 1936), p. 57, and Aristotle,
De partibus animalium, iv. 5. 681ª, 697ª⁻ᵇ, on sponges and bats, *De generatione animalium*,
761ª14, on *testacea*, between plants and shell-fish.

[3] See James Hutton, *The Greek Anthology in Italy to the Year 1800* (Cornell University Press, 1935), p. 60.

[4] The riddle *avis, nec tamen avis*, of the bat, attributed to Plato, is repeated by
Clearchus and Athenaeus. See Reusner, op. cit., 'Vespertilio'; for riddles by Sym-
posius, Hadrianus Junius, Claude Roselet, and Reusner himself; William Browne,
Bri annia's Pastorals, i. iv. 415, 'The two-kinde Bat'.

For the sponge see Reusner, *Aenigmatographia* (1602), especially J. C. Scaliger, p. 35,
but also Symposius, Lippius, and Reusner himself. Cf. Sylvester, ed. cit., p. 31, of
tadpoles, 'Half-dead, half-living; half a frog, half-mud'. For the crocodile's jaw as a
natural miracle see Hugh of St. Victor, *Patr. Lat.* clxxvi. 820A, translated by Thomas
Heywood, *The Hierarchie*, p. 307. For the elephant see Reusner, op. cit., p. 232,
Symposius' riddle.

PLATE I

LXXI.
MIHI TERRA LA-
CVSQVE.

Arbitrii jurisque mei sunt terra lacusque,
An non vel magno principe sum potior?

ÆLIA.

Joachim Camerarius, *Symbolorum et Emblematum Centuriae* [2nd edition],
IV, lxxi, Nuremberg, 1605

Parvis componere magna.

To compare small with great things.

2 · MUCH IN LITTLE

—◄-◄-◄-◄·⟪⟫·►-►-►—

The Silke-wormes and their Flies

THOMAS MOUFET (1553–1604) was a physician of some distinction who practised poetry in his spare time, a friend of the Sidney circle (he dedicated his poem, *The Silke-wormes and their Flies* (1599), to 'Marie Countesse of Penbrooke'), and of some of England's most eminent botanists and biologists. His own *Insectorum sive Minimorum Animalium Theatrum* (1634) was translated by J. Rowland as *The Theater of Insects* (1658).

It may have been during his travels in Italy in 1579 (mentioned in a gloss to his poem, p. 38) that he met with Marcus Hieronymus Vida's Latin poem *Bombycum Libri Duo* (Lyons and Basle, 1537). His own poem is not a strict imitation of Vida's georgic: he kept practical advice for the second book, and rejected his Ovidian myth of origins, after summarizing it, and other profane tales, such as the legend of Pyramus and Thisbe, for hexaemerai speculation (did the egg or the fly come first at creation?) and pious reflection. The poem is something of a sermon, abounding in devout and delightful commonplaces, and mingling useful instruction with traditional wisdom.

Little Things

DISWITTED dolts that huge things wonder at,
And to your cost coast daily ile from ile,
To see a Norway Whale, or Libian cat,
A Carry-castle, or a Crocodile,
If leane Ephesian or th'Abderian fat[1]
Liv'd now, and saw your madnesse but a while,
    What streaming flouds would gush out of theyr eies,
    To see great wittols little things despise?

When looke, as costliest spice is in small bagges,
And little springs so send forth cleerest flouds,
And sweetest *Iris* beareth shortest flagges,
And weakest *Osiers* bind up mighty woods,

[1] 'Heraclitus, that ever wept. Democritus, that ever laughed at the worlds folly.'

And greatest hearts make ever smallest bragges,[1]
And little caskets hold our richest goods:
   So both in Art and Nature tis most cleere,
   That greatest worths in smallest things appeare.

What wise man ever did so much admire
Neroes Colossus five score cubits hie,
As Theodorus Image cast with fire,[2]
Holding his file in right hand hansomly,
In left his paire of compasses and squire,
With horses, Coach, and footmen running by
   So lively made, that one might see them all?
   Yet was the whole worke than a flie more small.

Nay, for to speake of things more late and rife,
Who will not more admire those famous Fleas,
Made so by art, that art imparted life,
Making them skippe, and on mens hands to seaze,
And let out bloud with taper-poynted knife,
Which from a secret sheathe ranne out with ease:[3]
   Then those great coches which themselves did drive,
   With bended scrues, like things that were alive?

Ingenious Germane,[4] how didst thou convey
Thy Springs, thy Scrues, thy rowells, and thy flie?
Thy cogs, thy wardes, thy laths, how didst thou lay?
How did thy hand each peece to other tie?
O that this age enjoy'd thee but one day,
To shew thy Fleas to faithlesse gazers eye!
   That great admirers might both say and see,
   In smallest things that greatest wonders bee.

---

[1] M. P. Tilley, A Dictionary of Proverbs in England in the Sixteenth and Seventeenth Centuries (Michigan, 1950), O 3, Oaks may fall when reeds stand the storm; H 312, The Heart of a fool is in his tongue.

[2] Pliny, Historia Naturalis (Loeb Classical Library), XXXIV, xix.

[3] 'Made by Gawen Smith, Anno, 1586.'

[4] Du Bartas set the fashion of praising remarkable automata in verse (Sylvester, ed. cit., pp. 134–5), with special reference to Architas' dove and Regiomontanus. His 'flie' is a popular creature. See Bishop Wilkins, Mathematicall Magick (1648), II. vi; Sir Thomas Browne, Religio Medici (1642), I. xv; Gaspar Schott, Magia universalis Naturae et artis (1657), i. 22. For nature's ingenuities, see Michael Piccard, 'De Lusibus ... Naturae' in Dornavius, Amphitheatrum, pp. 181–4.

Great was that proud and feared Philistine,
Whose launces shaft was like a weavers beame,
Whose helmet, target, bootes, and brigandine,
Weare weight sufficient for a sturdy teame,
Whose frowning lookes and hart-dismaying eyne,
Daunted the tallest king of *Israels* realme:
    Yet little shepheard with a pibble stone,
    Confounded soone that huge and mighty one.

Huge fiery Dragons, Lions fierce and strong
Did they such feare on cruel Tyrant bring,
With bloudy teeth or tailes and talens long,
With gaping Jawes or double forked sting,
As when the smallest creepers ganne to throng,
And seize on every quicke and living thing?
    No, no. The Egyptians never feared mice,
    As then they feared little crawling lice.

Did ever Piseus[1] sound his trumpet shrill
So long and cleere, as doth the summer Gnat,
Her little cornet which our eares doth fill,
Awaking ev'n the drowsiest drone thereat?
Did ever thing do *Cupid*[2] so much ill,
As once a Bee which on his hand did squat?
    Confesse we then in small things vertue most,
    Gayning in worth what they in greatnesse lost.

But holla, Muse, extol not so the vale,
That it contemne great hilles, and greater skie,
Thinke that in goodnesse nothing can be small,
For smalnesse is but an infirmitie,
Natures defect, and offspring of some fall,
The scorne of men, and badge of infamy?
    For still had men continued tall and great,
    If they in goodnesse still had kept their seate.

[1] 'A most famous trumpeter. Pliny.'
[2] 'Anacreon in one of his latter Odes.'

A little dismall fire whole townes hath burnd,
A little winde, doth spread that dismall fire,
A little stone a carte hath overturnde,
A little weede hath learned to aspire,
The little Ants (in scorne so often spurnd)
Have galles: and flies have seates of fixed ire.
    Small Indian gnattes have sharpe and cruel stings,
    Which good to none, but hurt to many brings.[1]

And truely for my part I list not prayse
These silke-worme-parents for their little sise,
But for those lovely great resplendant rayes,
Which from their woorks and worthie actions rise,
Each deede deserving well a Crowne of bayes,
Yea, to be graven in wood that never dies:
    For let us now recount their actions all,
    And truth wil prove their vertues are not small.

The mulberry

O PEERELESSE tree, whose wisedome is far more
Then any else that springs from natures wombe:
For though *Pomonaes* daughters[2] budde before,
And forward *Phillis*[3] formost ever come,
And *Persian*[4] fruit yeeldes of her blossoms store,
And *Taurus*[5] hotte succeedeth *Aries* roome:
    Yet all confesse the Mulbery most wise,
    That never breedes till winter wholly dies.

---

[1] See Tilley, *A Dictionary of Proverbs*, F 274, A little Fire burns up a great deal of corn; W 424, A little Wind kindles, much puts out the fire; S 884, A little Stone in the way overturns a great wain; W 238, An ill Weed grows apace; F 393, The Fly has her spleen, and the ant her gall (Erasmus, *Adagia*; Lyly, *Euphues and his England*); V 67, No Viper so little but has its venom.

[2] 'All kinde of round fruit.'

[3] 'The Almonde tree.'

[4] 'Peaches: brought first out of Persia, as Columella writeth.'

[5] Taurus and Aries are the signs of April and March.

Such is her wit: but more her inward might,
For budded newe when *Phoebus* first appeares,
She is full leaved e're it grow to night:
With wondrous crackling filling both our eares,
As though one leafe did with another fight,
Striving who first shall see the heav'nly spheares,
    Even as a lively chickin breakes the shell,
    Or blessed Soules do scudde and flie from hell.

Yet witte and strength her pittie doth exceede,
For none she hurts that neere or under grow,
No not the brire, or any little weede,
That upwards shootes, or groveling creepes below,
Nay more, from heavenly flames each tree is freed
That nigh her dwels, when fearful lightnings glow:
    For vertue which, the Romanes made a law,
    To punish them that should her cut or saw.

Transformation

But wil you know, why this they onely eate?[1]
Why leaves they onely chuse, the fruite forsake?
Why they refuse al choise and sortes of meate,
And hungers heate with onely one dish slake?
Then list a while, you wonder-seekers great,
Whilst I an answere plaine and easie make:
    Disdaine you not to see the mighty ods,
    Twixt vertuous worms and sinful humane gods.

I thinke that God and nature thought it meete,
The noblest wormes on noblest tree to feede:
And therefore they else never set their feete
On any tree that beareth fruit or seede:
Others divine, that they themselves did weete
No other tree could yeelde their silken threede.

---

[1] Samuel Daniel, *The worthy tract of Paulus Jovius . . . called Imprese* (1585), describes an emblem of a silkworm on a mulberry-bush, with the motto from Petrarch, 'Suol di vivo, e d'altremi calpoco', representing love's exclusiveness.

Judge learned wittes: But sure a cause there is,
Why they else feede upon no tree but this.

. . . . .

Wherefore as soone as they beginne to creepe,
Like sable-robed Ants, farre smaller tho,
Black at the first, like pitch of Syrian deepe,
Yet made in time as white as *Atlas* snow,
Send servants up to woods and mountaines steepe,
When Mulb'ry leaves their maiden lippes do shew:
   Feede them therewith (no other soule they crave,
   If morne and ev'n fresh lefage they may have).

The first three weekes the tend'rest leaves are best,
The next, they crave them of a greater size,
The last, the hardest ones they can disgest,
As strength with age increasing doth arise:
After which time all meate they do detest,
Lifting up heads, and feete, and breast to skies,
   Begging as t'were of God and man some shrowde,
   Wherein to worke and hang their golden clowde.

Thus being kept and fed nine weekes entire,
Surpriz'd with age ere one would thinke them yong,
With what an ardent zeale and hot desire
To recompence thy travels do they long?
They neither sleepe, nor meate, nor drinke require,
But presse and strive, yea fiercely strive and throng,
   Who first may find some happy bough or broom,
   Whereon to spinne and leave their amber loome.[1]

Then virgins then, with undefiled hand
Sever the greatest from the smaller crue,
For al alike in age like ready stand,
Now to begin their rich and oval clue,

[1] The spinning of the silkworm was given praise in verse by Thomas Stanley, 'This silkworm to long sleep retired', by Henry Tubbe, *Poems* (ed. from MS. by G. C. Moore Smith, 1915), 'Pretty neat Huswife', and by Barten Holyday, *A Survey of the World* (1661) ii. 145-6. Peacham, *Minerva Britanna* (1612), lxxxix, contrasts the profitable weaving of the worm with man's unprofitable efforts.

(Having first paid as Nature doth command,
To bellies-farmer that which was his due)
For nothing must remaine in body pent,
Which may defile their sacred monument.

So being clensde from al that is impure,
Put each within a paper-coffin fine,
Then shal you see what labour they endure,
How farre they passe the weavers craft of line,
What cordage first they make and tackling sure,
To ty thereto their bottom most divine,
 Rounding themselves ten thousand times and more,
 Yet spinning stil behind and eke before.

Go gallant youths, and die with gallant cheere,[1]
For other bodyes shortly must you have,
Of higher sort then you enjoyed here,
Of worthier state, and of a shape more brave,
Lie but three weekes within your silken beere,
Till Syrian dogge be drownd in westerne wave,
 And in a moment then mongst flying things,
 Receive not feete alone, but also wings.

---

[1] For Joachim Camerarius (*Symbolorum et Emblematum Centuriae*, Nuremberg, 1590–1604, III. xcv) the silkworm's life was an emblem of conversion from a life of youthful pleasure to studious maturity. His picture shows the fly emerging from its cocoon, with the motto, 'Purus ut erumpam'. For Jacob Cats also, in *Silenus Alcibiadis* (Middelburgh, 1618), it represented spiritual resurrection. His poem, 'Ecce nova omnia' was translated by Thomas Heywood, *The Hierarchie*, pp. 616–17:

> A meere trunke was the Silke-worme, now it flies,
> A white Bird sporting in th'Ambrosiall Skies.
> Before a Worme: What a great change is here!
> Of the first shape no semblance doth appeare.
> Garments, Wealth, Banquets, Contracts, Mannors, Joy,
> Love, Language, Fellowship, *Change* must destroy.
> Such men whom Divine ardor doth inspire,
> Must of this terrhene drosse quench all desire.

Cf. Henry Vaughan, *The Mount of Olives* (1652), in *Works*, ed. L. C. Martin, p. 177, and *Silex Scintillans* (1655), 'Resurrection and Immortality', p. 400. See also R. Hughey and P. Hereford, 'Elizabeth Grymeston and her *Miscellanea*' (*Library*, xv, 1934).

PLATE II

226

EMBLEMA

AMOR ELEGANTIÆ PATER.

MORALE.

Claud.

Asperius nihil est humili, cum surgit in altum.

Senec.

Fortuna nimis quem fovet, stultum facit.

SACRVM.

2 Corinth. 5, 17.

SI quis sit in Christo, nova sit creatura, vetera transierunt, ecce! nova facta sunt omnia.

Ephes. 4, 22.

DEspouillez le viil homme, quant à la conversation precedente, & soyez renouvellés en l' esprit, revestus du nouvel homme.

Lieven

Jacob Cats, *Silenus Alcibiadis*, Amsterdam, 1630

Wings whiter then the snow of Taurus hie,
Feete fairer then *Adonis* ever had,
Heads, bodies, breasts, and necks of Ivory,
With perfit favour, and like beautie clad,
Which to commend with some varietie,
And shadow as it were with colour sad,
   Two little duskie feathers shall arise
   From forehead white, to grace your Eben eyes.

Then neither shall you see the bottom move,
Nor any noyse perceive with quickest eare,
Death rules in all, beneath, in midst, above,
Wherefore make haste you damsels voyd of feare,
Shake off delay, as ere you profit love,
In boxes straite away your bottoms beare,
   Freed from the coffin wherin late they wrought,
   To gaine the golden fleece you so much sought.

The silk-industry[1]

AND thou whose trade is best and oldest too,
Steward of all that ever Nature gave,
Without whose help what can our rulers doo,
Though gods on earth appareld wondrous brave?
Behold thy helping hand faire virgins wooe,
Yea nature bids, and reason eake doth crave
   Thy cunning, now these little worms to nurse,
   Which shal in time with gold fill full thy purse.

In steed of fruitles elms and sallowes gray,
Of brittle Ash, and poyson-breathing ugh,
Plant Mulb'ry trees nigh every path and way,
Shortly from whence more profit shal ensue,

---

1 Around 1600 there were hopes for an English silk-industry which led to the translation of D'Olivier de Serres' treatise, *The Perfect Use of silke-wormes, and their benefit* (1607), by Nicholas Geffe, with an address to James I and an introductory poem by Michael Drayton. Peacham addressed his emblem to William Stallenge, who, he claims, was 'first Author of making Silke in our Land'.

Then from th'Hesperian wood, or orchards gay,
On every tree where golden apples grew:
   For what is silke but ev'n a Quintessence,
   Made without hands beyond al humane sense?

A quintessence? nay wel it may be call'd,
A deathlesse tincture, sent us from the skies,
Whose colour stands, whose glosse is ne're appalld,
Whose Mulbr'y-sent and savour never dies,
Yea when to time all natures else be thralld,
And every thing Fate to corruption ties:
   This onely scornes within her lists to dwell,
   Bettring with age, in colour, glosse, and smel.

Pleasure from silk-worms

CONCERNING pleasure: who doth not admire,
And in admiring, smiles not in his hart,
To see an egge a worme, a worme a flier,
Having first shewd her rare and peerelesse art,
In making that which princes doth attire,
And is the base of every famous Mart?
   And then to see the flie cast so much seede,
   As doth, or may, an hundred spinsters breede.

Againe to view uppon one birchen shredde,
Some hundred Clewes to hang like clustred peares,
Those greene, these pale, and others somewhat red,
Some like the locks hanging downe *Phoebus* eares:
And then, how Nature when each worme is dead,
To better state in tenne dayes space it reares:
   Who sees all this, and tickleth not in minde,
   To marke the choyse and pleasures in each kinde.

Eye but their egges, (as Grecians terme them well)
And with a penne-knife keene divide them quite,
Behold their white, their yolke, their skin, and shel,
Distinct in colour, substance, forme, and sight:

And if thy bodies watchmen do not swell,
And cause thee both to leape and laugh outright,
  Thinke God and Nature hath that eye denied,
  By which thou shouldst from brutish beasts be tried.

When they are worms, mark how they color change,
From blacke to browne, from browne to sorrel bay,
From bay to dunne, from dunne to duskie strange,
Then to an yron, then to a dapple gray,
And how each morne in habites new they range,
Till at the length they see that happy day,
  When (like their Sires and heau'nly angels blest)
  Of pure and milk-white stoles they are possest.

Lay then thine eare and listen but a while,
Whilst each their foode from leafage fresh receaves,
Trie if thou canst hold in an outward smile,
When both thine eare and phantasie conceaves,
Not worms to feed, but showrings to distil,
In whispring sort upon the tatling leaves:
  For such a kind of muttring have I heard,
  Whilst herbage greene with unseene teeth they teard.

When afterward with needle pointed tongue,
The Flies have bor'd a passage through their clewes,
Observe their gate and steerage al along,
Their salutations, couplings, and *Adieus*:
Heare eke their hurring and their churring song,
When hot *Priapus* love and lust renewes,
  And tel me if thou heardst, or e're didst eye,
  Like sport amongst all winged troupes that flye.[1]

[1] The silkworm represents the follies and woes of love in Marino's 'Bombice d'amore', translated by Drummond as 'A daedale of my death', in Browne's 'Fido: an Epistle to Fidelia', and in Margaret Cavendish's *Nature's Pictures* (1656), pp. 84–85. Cf. Moufet, p. 19:

> That still we make our love our winding sheete,
> Whilst more we love, or hotter then is meete.

Tis likewise sport to heare how man and maide,
Whilst winding, twisting, and in weaving, thay
Now laugh, now chide, now scan what others saide,
Now sing a Carrol, now a lovers lay,
Now make the trembling beames to cry for aide,
On clattring treddles whilst they roughly play:
   Resembling in their rising and their falls,
   A musicke strange of new found *Claricalls.*[1]

The smel likewise of silken wool that's new,
To heart and head what comfort doth it bring,
Whilst we it wind and tooze from oval clew;
Resembling much in prime of fragrant spring,
When wild-rose buds in greene and pleasant hue,
Perfume the ayre, and upward sents do fling,
   Well pleasing sents, neither too sowre nor sweete,
   But rightly mixt, and of a temper meete.

As for the hand, looke how a lover wise
Delighteth more to touch *Astarte* slick
Then *Hecuba*, whose eye-browes hide her eies,
Whose wrinckled lippes in kissing seeme to prick,
Vpon whose palmes such warts and hurtells rise,
As may in poulder grate a nutmegge thick:
   So joy our hands in silke, and seeme ful loth
   To handle ought but silke and silken cloth.

Such are the pleasures, and farre more then these,
Which head, and hart, eies, eares, and nose, and hands,
Take, or may take, in learning at their ease,
The dieting of these my spinning bands,
Whose silken threede shal more then counterpeise,
Paine, cost, and charge, what ever it us stands,
   So that if gaine or pleasure can perswade,
   Go we, let us learne the silken staplers trade.

[1] *Claricalls:* clavichord.

The Bee and the Marigold

'T. CUTWODE', that is, the courtier Tailboys Dymoke (as Leslie Hotson has established, 'Marigold of the Poets', *Transactions of the Royal Society of Literature*, New Series, xvii, 1938), was not an altogether tasteful or polished writer in his poem *Caltha Poetarum: Or, The Bumble Bee* (1599); yet he had an eye for a new fashionable mode, in which insects, floral ladies, and a rather unbridled set of deities mingle together. In his address 'To the conceited Poets of our age' Dymoke described his poem as a mixture of the pastoral and the erotic. 'Gentlemen & others, I pray you let us holde together for the preservation of our reputation, and maintain the prescription of our lowe subjects, least *Apollos* musick do quite drown poore *Pan*, and the countrey Hornpipe be laid aside.'

The story is of Venus' displeasure at the coldness of the marigold's responses to her admirer, the woodbine, and of Cupid's arrow which misses the marigold and hits a visiting bee. The bee becomes the flower's devotee, to Venus' greater annoyance. Cupid is commanded to capture it, and is stung, while the bee escapes. Caltha is rescued in the nick of time by Diana, and turned into a maiden; but Venus arranges a wedding between the primula and a mandrake, and punishes the bees. Caltha's bee-admirer becomes a wandering hermit and arrives at Diana's grove, is recognized, turned into a man, and goes to the primula's wedding to take his revenge on Venus.

Though Hotson makes a strong claim that the poem is a riddle of courtly intrigue, it is most readable where this is secondary to story-telling for its own sake.

The Marigold

I

MY Herball booke in Folio I unfold,
    I pipe of Plants, I sing of sommer flowers,
But chiefly of the Mayden Marygold,
    and of the Daisie, both brave Belamours:
Trophies for Kings, Imprese for Emperours,
    Garlands to beare upon the brave Ensignes
Of Knights, of Peeres, of princely Palladines.

* * *

18

The next my pretie Marygold displaies,
    her golden bloome like to the sunny beames

Spreading abroad her rich and radyent rayes,
    resembling *Titan* in his hottest streames,
Even in the glory of his Summer gleames:
So shynes my Marygold, so doth she showe,
So as she seemes a second Sun belowe.

19

Who in the morning spreads her yealow haire
    like to the blaze of golden *Phœbus* bright
That maks the hevenly clymes to shine so clear,
    illuminating all the world with light,
So shines my Marygold so faire in sight:
Till in the darke when as the day is dun,
She closeth up and setteth with the Sun.

20

Thus proudly doth she brave sir *Phebus* shining
    and seconds him both in his prime of morn,
And in the night even at his downe declining,
    setting the silly Sunburnt god at scorn,
As if that she the soveraigne sway had born,
Disdaining things inferiour here that lies:
But lookes aloft, as Ladie of the Skies.

21

On her attends the Dasie dearly dight,
    that pretie Primula of Lady *Ver*,
As hand-maid to her mistresse day and night,
    so doth she watch, so waiteth she on her,
With double diligence and dares not stir,
A fairer flower perfumes not forth in May,
Then is this Daisie, or this Primula.

22

About her neck she wears a rich wroght ruffe,
    with double sets most brave & broad bespread,

Resembling lovely Lawn or Cambrick stuffe,
  pind up and pricke upon her yealow head,
Wearing her haire on both sides of her shead:
And with her countenance she hath a cast,
Wagging the wanton with each wynd and blast.

23

Commend me to the yong ones of the Corte,
  and marke how as the pretie Mophies[1] sits,
Wagging their countenance in seemely sorte,
  with modest blush that bewtie so befits,
Wyeling fond lovers sometime from their wits:
So wags this wanton with a red complexion,
When as the Sun darts to her his reflection.

24

Heere could I set you downe the Honysuckle
  the pretie Pinke and purple Pianet,
The Bugles, Boradge, and the blew Bottle,
  the bonny Belamour and Violet,
And thriving Thrift if men would gather it
With lovely Lillies and the faire Narcis,
And *Venus* sleepe at noone with *Adonis*.

Cupid's aim

36

THIS cunning Archer aymeth at the marke
  (mary at hittie missie is he tooting)
The Boy was blind as is the dazled darke,
  and never suer, nor certaine in his shooting:
For oftentimes he fayleth in his footing.
As you shall heare how this same craftie child,
Even in the brag of cunning was beguild.

[1] 'Moppe': ' a little prety lady, or tender young thing' (Puttenham).

37

It chanct, a Bee came flying to this flower,
  with humming melodie, & bumming noyce:
And lights upon her stalk even at that stower,
  for in his flowers he is very choyce:
Sitting & singing there with buzing voyce.
Working in sommer for his healthfull hive,
That he in winter might the better thrive.

38

He came but lately from the damaske Rose,
  Unto my Marygould that shines so sunnie:
And got him there a paire of yealow hose,
  of virgin waxe, all wet about with hunnie.
The sweetest wax that can be made for mony
With Meldeaw clam'd and clagged were his knees,
To cary home, & bring unto his Bees.

39

But walladay, he was not there aware,
  of *Cupids* shaft, nor of his sudden clap:
The Hony catcher came unto his care,
  for there the silly flie received a rap:
(Alas poore Bumble buz, for thy ill hap)
For why the blinded boy (ay me for thee)
Did misse the golden bud, and gauld the Bee.

40

But here I leave the honey bird confounded,
  that wofully aloft away did fling:
All unto death he is most deeply wounded,
  and stung himself, that somtimes us'd to sting:
Here must I leave that hony bird of wing,
And tell how *Venus* waxed wrathfull wilde,
And red with anger at her recklesse childe.

A plea for the Marigold

46

To this her *Cupid* answered pretely,
  how often (mother) have I seene you shake
The beawtie and the splendor of this tree,
  and of the Marygoulds, gay garlands make:
Yea you your self to weare them for their sake.
And on your locks to place the pretie ones,
Preferring them before the precious stones.

47

How often have I seene your Coatcher trot,
  when you in pomp to *Paphos* Island ran?
How often (mother) have I garlands got,
  for every Dove, and every milk white Swan
That drew your Chariot & your gay waggan.
And make your prety Pidgions teams & yoaks
Of Mary-goulds to hang about their throats.

48

How often have the buds bene laid abroad
  upon the traces whereas you should tread?
How oft have they thy stately altars strawd,
  and we exalting there thy holy head,
Whilst *Hymnes* wer sung, & sacred Psalms were sed:
Me thinks I see how all the rabble runs,
Unto thy Church, with chaines of golden suns.

49

Then (queen) accept the offsprings of this flower,
  and offer not the golden Bud disgrace,
For she is pleasing to thy princely power,
  and therefore curse it not in any case:
I pray thee mother let my prayers take place,
And let her shine as doth the glimpsing sunne,
And do as well as she tofore hath done.

50

Thus *Cupid* said, but see this self-wild wench,
   Venus she brings a Brierhooke in her hand,
And cuts me down each border & green bench
   and all the shading shelter that did stand,
To guard the flowers from the filchers hand,
And letteth in a Northern uncouth aire,
That almost blasted had her Bloomes so faire.

The bee's wooing

53

BUT now I will returne unto the Bee,
   the little Wasp and sillie wounded thing:
Who like a souldier from the victorie,
   comes maymed home, his arme upon a string:
So droups this Bee, so hangs he down his wing,
Shewing the Marygold his mortall scarre,
Who unto death was wounded in her warre.[1]

*   *   *

56

Unto this flower he falles downe on his knee,
   just at the roote that grew upon the ground:
And said grant mercie Marygold on me,
   and lend a leafe to lay unto my wound,
That it might plaister me and make me sound.
For on thy branch I here did take my bane,
And here I hope to be recured againe.

57

Denie me not (oh thou faire golden flower)
   sweet give mee leave a while that I might sit

---

[1] For the bee-soldier see William Drummond, 'As an audacious knight' (*Poetical Works*, ed. L. E. Kastner, Edinburgh, 1913, i. 112), from Tasso, and Marvell, 'Upon Appleton House', st. xl.

Upon thy yealow head and worke an hower,
  and for my hungry se'fe some honey get,
For all is wasted, I have not a whit.
I tell thee my distresse, to thee I shrive me,
I have no helpe, unlesse thy selfe wilt hive me.

58

I will not (as the creeping canker) waste thee,
  nor as the worm in woodsear time bespew thee,
I come not like the Butterflie to blast thee:
  nor with foule deadly venom to bedeawe thee:
Ile leave thee even as fresh as earst I knew thee:
Ile make my golden shrub that shines so sunny,
As sweet as is the hony combe or hunny.

59

With that (but I must tell you here a wonder)
  and almost past my credit for to speake,
This branch her biggen[1] she did burst in sunder
  her haire upon a sudden on her neck,
That seemd to wave, and give the Bee a back:
And laid her leaves wide open there for him,
That up aloft the Bee might better climb.

*   *   *

61

There he receives the deaw of hony drops,
  and bathes his lims that were so leane & lank,
And in her circle up and downe he hops,
  and feeds apace and doth refresh his flank,
And with her wax he stores his spindle shank,
And now the hony bird away doth styve,
With bumming and with humming to his hyve.

[1] *Biggen*, cap.

62

To buz of *Caltha* now the Bee was bold,
    of *Caltha* now were all the Echos ringing:
For now no more he cals her Marygold,
    but newes from Lady *Caltha* is he bringing,
Of faire sweet Lady *Caltha* is he singing:
And up and downe he flieth with her fame,
Till he unto his hive and harbour came.

63

His Bees with welcome round about him swarms
    and bringeth him into his thatched home,
And marching all along like men at armes,
    they place him in the highest hony come,
Where he as king doth keepe, and rules alone,
And all his subjects offering him their service:
For to disarme him of his hony harnies.

64

One doth his boots unbutton from his shins,
    an other helps for to untie his hose:
An other wipeth hony from his wings,
    that came from Lady *Caltha* and the rose,
The which he gets when he his prograce goes.
And thus comd home with hevie drowsy hed,
Th'unnumbred birds do bring their Bee to bed.

65

And there he sleeps & slumbers til the morne,
    when he awakes and wipes his pinking eies,
And up he starts and bloweth like a horne,
    where all his souldiers in a swarme do rise,[1]
Attending on him wheresoever he flies.
And he againe into his garden goes,
Wherein his Goddesse Lady *Caltha* growes.

[1] See *Georgics* iv, watchmen-bees at the hive door 'onera accipiunt venientium'; the new arrivals have 'crura thymo plenae'.

66

There sit they round about & gards this flower
  some making of their hony on the Mallow:
An other biting on the Bellamour,
  an other like a little dapper fellow
Worketh on yarrow, making wax so yealow,
And every Fly unto his flower goes,
Some to the Red, some to the damask Rose.

67

Where having got their hony and their wax,
  they come to *Caltha*, where their maister sits,
And throws their hony Jerkins down & Jacks
  and gives to him the gaine their labour gets.
Thus industrie his common welth befits:
So when they are disloded of their store,
They buz about, and flies away for more.

68

In meane while this same mightie bumble Bee,
  is framing of a Chappell for his Queene,
With strange and costly Archetectury,
  the rarest sight that ever yet was seene,
Of waxen worke, was never like I weene:
Pillers of hony combes with Piramis,
And strong pilasters of great statelinesse.

69

And at one end there stands a proper steeple,
  dawbing his height with hony for his lime;
And bels to ring in these same pretie people,
  when as they take it to be service time,
To say their praiers, their Mattens & their prime
And when this Chappell ended was and wald,
La santa Caltha, this same bee it cald.

The bee's sting

78

To *Caltha* is the craftie Spyder gone,[1]
& weaveth there a witching web (god wot)
With subtle slender thrids and many a one,
    where if thou goest, thy chance is to be got,
What Flye soever comes escapes it not:
And let him toyle to come out of his gin,
The more he strives, the surer is he in.

79

The Cranion cast his net upon this flower,
    that seemed like a wroght branch under Lawn
And there it had not bene above an houre,
    but comes the Bee, and to this bud is flowne,
(He had not made such hast if he had knowne)
But after wit hath very seldome thanks,
The Bee is got & shakled by the shanks.

80

Now *Venus* figgeth,[2] and in hast she runs,
    and *Cupid* following after her doth fling:
And to this litle captive prisoner comes,
    whereas she takes the bumble by the wing:
(For why she was afraid the bee would sting)
And piniond him that nowhere could he pas,
But there as prisoner unto *Venus* was.

81

She bids her boy, that wily wanton wag,
    to hold him fast, least he should flie away:
Whilest she had tyde a thrid about his leg,
    and gave him *Cupid* for to find him play:
As children do with litle birds they say.

---

[1] The bee's traditional enemy was the spider: Hadrianus Junius, *Emblemata* (Antwerp, 1565), xxxiii; Spenser, *Amoretti*, lxxi.
[2] *Figgeth* (dial.), rushes.

And there the string he holdeth in his hand,
Whilest that the bee is buzzing in the band.

82

The boy he gave the bumble too much scope,
  he found such pretie gambals with the fly:
The Bee that had large compasse of his rope,
  flew at his face, and stung him by and by:[1]
Whereat poore *Cupid* he began to cry.
And from his fist the joyfull bird is fled,
And from aloft, with string about his leg.

83

He durst not flie where briers and bushes were,
  least that the thrid shuld trap him in the trees,
But mounts aloft and hovers in the Ayre,
  till that he came unto his little Bees,
That helps to pull the shackles from his knees.
And there Ile leave him sure and safe at home,
And tell how *Venus* doth her boy bemone.

84

She up and downe the Garden now doth gad,
  to gather all the coolest hearbs that grow:
To phisick and to leach her wounded lad,
  whose face like to a blather blown doth show:
As scarce his mother could her *Cupid* know.
And trying many precious plants that bee,
At length she cometh to the woodbind tree.

85

And going to his binding branch, that clung
  like to a Serpent twining on a tree:

---

[1] The classical sources of this incident are Theocritus, *Idylls*, xix, and Anacreon, *Carmina*, xxxv. See James Hutton, 'Cupid and the Bee' (*P.M.L.A.* lvi, 1941), J. C. Fucilla, 'Cupid and the Bee: Addenda' (ibid. lviii, 1943).

She told him, *Cupid* with a Bee was stung,
　　asking the flouer what phisick ther might bee
To take away the stinging of the flee.
Who answered her like to a learned Clark,
Bending with reverence, both his rynd & bark.

86

And said in phisick I have had some toyle,
　　and for the Scorpions stinging I have found.
Nothing can cure, but even his proper oyle,
　　which being taken, salves and maketh sound.
And easeth straight the anguish of the wound.
So, for this Bee, the best and chiefest thing,
Is his owne hony, for to kill his sting.

　　　　★　　★　　★

89

But *Venus* puls his tree downe by the top,
　　and forth from this, his hollow horned flower
Much of his liquid Meldew there did drop,
　　that shedded out a pretie hony shower,
Healing her *Cupid* with it that same houre:
And now her onely care, is how that she
Might be revenged on *Caltha* and the Bee.

The bee recognised

114

THE maister Bee into his garden goes,
　　to clense him from the filth of this same Fus,
And there he thinketh yet that *Caltha* growes
　　but thou art now deceiv'd (poor bumble buz)
That flower with faire *Dian* is gone from us:
And in her place he spies a Mandrag spring:
And now poore Bee, thy sorrowes do begin.

115

He voweth now for to forsake his hive,
  and like a Pilgrim spend his latter daies:
(Gods be his speed and send him wel to thrive)
  for now he meanes to wander uncoth waies,
And like an Hermit,[1] he himselfe arraies:
That safely he might wander up and downe,
And seek strange countries far, that be unknown.

116

He made himselfe a paire of holy beads,
  the fiftie Aves were of Gooseberies:
The Pater Nosters and the holy Creeds,
  were made of red & goodly fair ripe cheries:
Blessing his Marygold with Ave-maries.
And on a staffe made of a Fennell stalk,
The beadrowle hangs, whilest he along did walk.

117

And with the flower munkshood makes a coole
  and of a gray Dock got himselfe a gowne:
And looking like a Fox or holy foole,
  he barbs his litle beard, and shaves his crown,
And in his pilgrimage goes up & downe.
And with a Wabret[2] leafe he made a wallet,[3]
With scrip to beg his crums & pike his sallet.

★   ★   ★

119

And by the way, for sweete saint Charitie,
  he begs his largies of th'outlandish Hives:

---

[1] The bee stands more straightforwardly for the simple, devout life in *Howell his Devises* (1585), 'To his Friend E. R. of the Bee', and Henry Vaughan, *Thalia Redeviva* (1678), 'The Bee'. [2] *Wabret leafe* (dial.), plantain leaf.
[3] Two Cupids quarrel over the possession of the bee's bag in Herrick's *Hesperides* (1648), no. 92, in *Herrick's Poetical Works*, ed. L. C. Martin (Clarendon Press, Oxford, 1956), p. 31.

Where having had their liberalitie,
   they send him packing & the Droanbee drives
To beg and live amongst the idle lives:
And farre and neare, farther then I can tell,
He goes whereas the oughly Hornets dwell.

120

He passed through *Appuleia*, mongst the flyes,
   and to that country where the scorpions are:
And to a kingdome of *Camaradyes*,
   whereas the Gnats and biting gadflies were,
That feard, the bumblebee from biding there.
But with his bag and baggage is he gone,
Wandring the World in uncoths far unknowne.

121

At length he lights on famous *Ephesus*,
   where chaste *Diana* and her vestals bee,
And now full wearie flies to *Platanus*,
   an aged and an auncient hollow tree,
Where he must rest a while (poor fainting flee)
Precisely looking least the spider webs
Were lurking there to catch him by the legs.

122

Now having got his sleepe and quiet rest,
   his morning Mattins doth he buz and sing:
And being rowsed from his sluggish nest,
   with lauds and Letanies aloft doth fling,
And flieth now abroad with burgond wing,
And saieth his Psalmists in his sursarare,
With *Pater Noster*, and with *Avie Marie*.

123

And whilest this runnagate about did rove,
   it hapned that by chance he did repaire,

Unto a gladsome and a goodly Grove,
　whereas *Diana* and her vestals were,
And *Caltha* too (unknowne to him) was there
Where all the traine assembled in that place,
For to attend and guard *Diana's* grace.

124

Some sits them down & gathereth green bushes
　and others very busie do begin:
To weave their litle baskets of Bulrushes,
　to put their hearbs & all their flowers in:
Least that they scatter them in gathering.
An other daintily her selfe doth deck,
With garlands for to weare about her neck.

125

Som makes their springs & pitfals for the thrush
　and very busie round about they stird:
An other lasse she comes and beats the bush,
　and by your leave, an other takes the bird:
And sport alone, for Lady and for Lord.
And in a Cage that he must learne to sing,
But soft and faire, not till the next year spring.

126

There Lady *Caltha* in her lap she holds,
　and had her skirt her Apron full and all,
Of double Dasies and of Marygolds,
　and there she pins and pricks them on her Call:
(Now fine and feate and faire might she befal)
For on her locks the flowers stick and stay,
Even for her selfes sake, and faire *Primula*.

127

The Bee no sooner spies these Marygolds,
　but to the yealow flowers he is fled:

And lights upon her locks that lay in rowles,
   buzing & huzing round about her head:
Till at the length he sits upon her shead.
But there faire *Caltha* would not let him stay,
For with a bush, she beats the Bee away.

128

Yet from the Marygolds he would not flie,
   nor from her presence will he so depart:
Although by them first came his miserie,
   and whylom wounded was unto the heart,
(As you have heard of late) throgh *Cupids* dart.
Yet would he not away, but busie there,
The Bee is buzing round about her eare.

129

Whereat faire *Caltha* strikes him to the ground,
   and hits the Fly full often with her fist:
The bumble Bee would up againe rebound,
   and be upon her head ere she had wist:
Then would she strike againe, and oft she mist.
Whereat the Ladies they would laugh to see,
What sport there was, twixt *Caltha* & the Bee.

130

But as the Fly that with the candle mocks,
   and plaies so long til he hath burnt his wings,
So is this Bee entangled in her locks,
   and fetterd in these golden yealow strings,
And by the feet he in her trammels hings.
And now the Lady *Caltha* she doth crie,
Whilest that *Diana* comes to catch the Flie.

131

The bird now taken from her golden locks,
   faire *Caltha* is desirous of the Fly,

And takes the Bee, and puts him in a box,
    and cals for hony for him presently,
And makes his bed of Roses by and by:
And Marygolds with pillowes of the Dasie,
That he might lie full lither[1] and full lazie.

132

Whereat *Diana*, at Lady *Caltha* laught,
    & askt, what she wold do with that same droan
And said the slothful thing was good for naught,
    But for all that she lets the Bee alone,
And from her box she will not have him gone:
But there the pretie Fly he takes his rest,
Whilest that she told *Diana* this same jest.

133

Good Madam when I grew a garden flower,
    Venus and *Cupid* came to shoote at me:
And then it chanc't (sweet Lady) at that stower,
    I was defended by a litle Bee:
Who blest my branch from his artillerie.
And by good luck and fortune thither came,
To put the cunning Archer from his ayme.

134

For whilest the Bee was biting of my bloome,
    by chance my body up and downe he stird:
So that the Archer did at randome rome,
    and mist my branch and gauld the little bird:
(The bee was in the box & heard the word)
But forwards went they (thinking that the Flie
Had never heard this tale, nor bene so nie).

---

[1] *Lither* (dial.), idle.

135

Now ever since (good Madame) pardon me,
   of all the pretie little fooles that flie,
I love the best the hyved hony bee,
   and he shall be my bird, untill I die:
With all his noyce and humming harmonie.
And let the painted Butterflyes and Flees
Live where they list, Ile love the hony Bees.

136

With that she openeth the litle Coffer,
   and shakes a Marygold unto the Bee:
The Bumble nods his head, & makes an offer,
   & come bird com (quoth *Caltha*) come to me
With so ho ho, and wo ho ho cries she,
And whistled too, and chirped with her lips,
With that the Bee out of his box he skips.

137

And as the Hawke reclaimed from his nest,
   and being full well managed and mand,
He comes and flies to Lady *Calthas* fist,
   and takes the golden pray at her faire hand:
And on the top of this same flower doth stand.
Not offering once to flie from her away,
But subject to the Ladies lewre doth stay.

138

This prints a strange impression in her soule,
   this Simpathy betwixt her and the Bee:[1]
Did halfe perswade her, that this was the foule,
   and absolutely said, this is the Flee,
That saved my flower when *Cupid* shot at mee.

---

[1] For the bee's attraction to the lady, see Secundus, *Basia* (Utrecht, 1541), iv and xv; Angeriano, 'De Caelia, api & Amore', in *Delitiae CC Poetarum Italorum* (1608); William Drummond, 'O! do not kill that bee'; Carew, 'Upon a Mole in Celia's Bosom'; Herrick, *Hesperides*, no. 182, 'The Captiv'd Bee: or, The little Filcher', ed. cit., p. 71.

This said, *Diana* sware, that she would try,
And through her sacred art, transform the Fly.

139

Now doth she frame her metamorphosin,
    And with her blessed bookes of divination,
She commeth to transforme and conjure him,
    And strangely workes his transmutation,
Casting her just count of his constellation:
And suddenly the bumble Bee as than,
Did take the shape and very forme of man.

The Owl, the Bat, and the Mole

WILLIAM WARNER (1558?–1609) relieved the dreariness of his versified chronicle, *Albions England* (1586, enlarged 1602), from time to time with fables, which suited his conversational manner, touched with humour.

This fable is told to Perkin Warbeck's wife by a courtly suitor as a parable of her own husband's situation. It has Aesopic analogues, none of them precisely similar. Like a variety of creatures, the bat pretends to be a bird, then an animal, to save its skin. In Caxton's version (*The Fables of Esope*, 1484, III. iv) there is a war between animals and birds; in one continental edition, in which the Planudean Aesop is accompanied by Gabrias and a number of other works, the bat encounters a weasel (*Aesopi Phrygis Fabulae*, Leyden, 1609, cix, 'Vespertilio et Mustela'); in Camerarius's edition the enemy is a cat (*Fabulae Aesopi*, Nuremberg, 1588, cviii, 'Vespertilio et Feles'). Both fables appear in Thomas Blage, *A Schole of wise Conceytes* (1569), 10 and 366. The moral is directed against double-mindedness in politics. (Compare the emblems of Alciati, lxii, and of Camerarius, III. lxxxix.) The bat was a popular riddle-subject in antiquity and Renaissance riddlers continued the habit (see Aristotle, *De partibus animalium*, 697 a–b). The mole emblematically represents the ignorant, base-minded man (Camerarius, II. cxiv; Scot, *Phylomithie*, 'Unio').

The text of the fable is taken from the 1602 edition of *Albions England*, VII. xxxvii.

SUPPOSE (for so must be suppos'd) that Birdes and Beastes did
    speake:
The Cuckooe sometimes lov'd the Owle, and so with her did
    breake,

Then flew the Owle by day, so did the Cuckooe all the yeere,
So did the Swallow and the Batte: but howe it hapned heare.
The Cuckooe by the Swallow (then the Swallow was his Page)
Did send the Owle a sucking Mouse, a tydie[1] for the age:
The Bat (the Bat then serv'd the Owle) preferd the Bringer and
The Present to her Mistres sight, that in her Todd did stand.
My maister to your Owleship, quoth the Swallow, sends by me
This Modicum, desiring you to take the same in gree.
The Owle, that never till that day had tasted flesh of Mouse,
Had quickly lopte a Limbe or two, and feasteth in her house
The Swallow with a cursee of her then disgorged wheat:
When, talking of the daintie flesh, and elswhat, as they eate,
The Bat (then waiting at the boorde) fetcht sighes a two or
   three:
The Owle did aske the cause. And doe you aske the cause,
   quoth he,
Why thus I sigh when thus in sight my kindred murthred be?
My selfe was sometimes such, and such am still, save now
   I fly:
With that he freshly wept: and thus proceeded by and by.
  A fresh, quoth he, now comes to minde mine Auncestors
   ill hap,
Whom pride made praies to Kestrels, Kites, Cats, Weasels,
   Bate & trap:
My Grandsier (for wheare Nature failes in strength she adds in
   wit)
Was full of Science: But, insooth, he misapplied it.
The Weasell, Prince of Vermen (though besides a vertuous
   Beast)
By shrewdnes of my Grandsiers wit his Holes with hoords
   increaste,
And seem'd to conn him thankes, whom none besides had
   cause to thank
For Princes Favours often make the favored too cranke.[2]
Not only Mice, but Lobsters, Cats, and noble Vermen paide
In comming *Coram Nobis* for some crime against them laide.

---

[1] *Tydie*, good.   [2] *Cranke*, active.

PLATE III

89

L X X X I X.

INTER VTRVM-
Q V E.

Vita fugit lucem diræ male confcia culpæ,
Ut quæ avis à fero vefpere nomen habet.

Z   *V*ESPER-

Joachim Camerarius, *Symbolorum et Emblematum Centuriae* [1st edition],
III, lxxxix, Nuremberg, 1590

But, God, it is a world to see, when purposes be sped,
How Princes, having fatted Such, are with their fatnes fed.
The Weasel serv'd my Grandsier so, and every Vermen laught
To see himselfe in Snare that had in Snares so many caught.
Now also live some wylie Beasts, and fatly do they feede
Mongst Beasts of chace & birds of game, with lesse then need-
    full heed.
My Grandsier dead, my Father was in favour netthelesse,
Nor did his Father more than he for high Promotion presse:
And (though I say it) long time he deserved favors well,
For quayling Foe men, and at home such Vermen as rebell:
And for the same the Weasell did him mightily preferre:
But Honors made him haughtie, and his haughtines to erre.
I will be plaine, he waxt too prowd, and plotted higher drifts
Than fitted him, or fadged[1] well, for who have thriv'd by
    shifts?
Nor will I say (because his sonne) he wrong'd the Weasell, but
The Weasell died, and that that did succeede to shifts he put.
For which his Fathers Fortune did oretake him at the last:
Such fickelnesse in earthly pompe, which, flowing ebs as fast.
This double warning might have jekt unto my wit, but I
Did follow Kinde: Nay, more, I did importune Dis to fly,
And he did give me these blacke wings, resembling him that
    gave them,
A proper Gift, and hardly got, to shame me now I have them.
But know yee Dis? some Pluto him or Limbos God doe call,
Or, aptlier said, in Hell of divels the Chiefe and Principall:
And somewhat now of him and how I changed say I shall.
    I hapned on a Cranny, whilst my Mouse-daies lasted, which
I entring, wandred crooked Nookes and pathes as darke as pitch:
Theare, having lost my selfe, I sought the open aire in vaine,
Both wanting foode, & light, and life well neere through travels
    paine.
The Moole by chaunce did crosse my way, and (as ye know)
    her smell
Supplies her want of sight and serves her purpose full as well

---

[1] *Fadged*, fitted.

I heard a tracting sound, and, skar'd, my haire did stand upright,
Nor could I see, or fly, but feare and blesse me from a Spright:
She had me, hild me, questions of my being theare the cause,
And in meane while peruseth me with favourable clawes.
I was about to plead for life, when she prevents me thus:
Ha, Cosen Mouse, what Fortune gives this meeting heere to us?
Feare not my Sonne (I call thee Sonne because I love thee much)
Doe hold thy selfe as merry heere as in a Pantlers hutch.
What know'st not me? or see'st thou not? with that she leadeth
    me
Into an higher roome, wheare her to be mine Eame[1] I see.
I did my dutie, and my heart was lightned when mine eie
Encountered a friend whereas I made account to die.
Before me sets Shee Viands, and my stomache serv'd me well:
And, having fed, my Grandsiers and my Fathers ends I tell.
(For she enquires for them, ere I acquaint her what befell.)
The reverent Moole, then sighing, saide: ah, let no vermine
    thinke
That Fortune ever favors, or that friends will never shrinke:
I did fore-smell their loftie flight would cost them once a fall,
And therefore, Cosen, see thou be forwarned therewithall.
Heere seest thou me (I tell thee, though I prise not Gentry
    now,
Thine Eame, and of the elder house) that long agoe did vow
My selfe a Recluse from the world, and, celled under ground,
Least that the gould, the precious stones and pleasures here be
    found
Might happen to Corrupt my minde, for blindnes did I pray,
And so contemplatively heere I with contentment stay.
Admitte the Weasell graceth thee, the more he doth the more
The other Vermen will maligne, and envy thee therefore:
Himselfe, perhaps, will listen to thy ruine for thy store:
Or thou thy selfe, to mount thy selfe, maiest runne thy selfe a
    shore.
That Vermen that hath reason, and his own defects espies,
Doth seeme to have a soule, at least doth thrive by such surmies,

---

[1] *Eame*, elder relation.

For what is it but reason that humaine from brutish tries?
But man, or beast, neither hath troth that this for truth denies,
He hath enough that hath werewith pure Nature to suffies:
In overplus an overcharge for soule and body lies,
For Souldiers, Lawyers, Carrions, Theeves, or Casaulties a
    Prize,
His comber-minde that lives with it and leaves it when he dies,
From whom to catch it scarce his heire staies closing of his eies:
O wretched wealth, which who so wants no Fortune him
    envies.
Here maiest thou feast thee with a Maid, & here no Pickethanke[1]
    pries
Into thy life, nor words well spoke to ill unmeant applies:
No Flatterer to undermind: no tongue no ears for lies:
No gleaning from the Orphant: no oppressed widowes cries:
No bribes to give, no hands to take: no quarrelling for flies:
No wrongs to right: no lawes to breake, because no law that
    ties,
But what we lust we doe, nor doe nor lust badd enterprize,
And finde lesse want in Nature, than wits-want in Arts disguize:
Nor any heere in force, in friends, fraud, wealth, or wit affies:
O doe thou not so rich, so safe, and just a life despies:
Theare lacketh not of noble Births to star the courtly skies:
Nor want we Pollititians, thou maiest for thy Soule be wise:
Then leave thou matters of estate to States, I thee advise:
And rather sit thou safely still, than for a fall to rise.

    Not for Shee was my Elder or mine Eame, but for the place
I hild my peace, that would have sayd her Moolships minde
    was bace.
But she perceives me to dissent, and saieth, Cosen Mouse,
Doe as you like, you shall not finde a prison of my house:
Stay while you will, goe when you will, come and returne at
    pleasure,
And ever welcome: Vertue is an uncompelled Treasure.
This past, and thence passe we through deepe dark waies, save
    here & theare,

---

[1] *Pickethanke,* flatterer.

The vaines of gould and pretious stones made light in darke
    appeare:
Vaste Vaults as large as Iles we passe, great Rivers theare did
    flow,
Huge wormes & Monsters theare I saw, which none on earth
    do know.
On goe we, till I saw a glimps, and she heard noise of flame,
Then said shee praiers, bidding me to blesse me from the
    same.
I, musing, frain'd her meaning: She her meaning thus did tell.
That flaming Region, ever such (quoth she) is *Plutos* Hel:
All gould, all mettals, wealth, and pompe that nourish Mortals
    pride
Are hence and his, and hether they doe theare mis-Guiders gide:
He them inchaunteth, and the same inchaunt the folke on Earth,
Untill their dying dotage theare finds heere a living death.
Still nertheles I wisht to see the hellish Monarch *Dis*,
When he (more ready to be found then for our profite is)
Ore heard us, and unhid himselfe, and shinde in rich array,
And seem'd a glorious Angell, and full gently thus did say.
That slandrous blind bace-minded Moole, friend Mouse,
    deceives thee much,
And prates of me, of Hell, and Earth more than is so or such:
Beleeve her not, but rather do beleeve thine eyes, and see
If any earthly pleasure is untripl'd heere with mee.
Then shewde he sights (which since I found illusions to betray)
Of greater worth than Earth affords, or I have Art to say:
Nay, more, he bids me aske what so I would, and I should have it:
Then did I pause, bethinking what was rarest I might crave it.
My Holes were stor'd with corne and croomes, on Earth I
    walkt at will,
And in her Bowels now had seene indifferently my fill,
Upon it, nor within it, not sufficing to my pride,
I asked winges, scarce asked when they grew on either side.
    Short leave I tooke, & mounting left the Hell-god and the
    Moole,
And soared to the open Aire through many a sory hoole.

It was at Twilight, and the Birds were gone to roust, but I
(Inchaunted with the noveltie of flight) unweared flye,
And had the Sunne been up, I ween (such pride bewitcht my
    wit
To Egel-fie my selfe) I had assayd to soare to it:
Not seeing that my limber wings were Leather-like unplum'de,
But at the Dawning also I of winge-worke still presum'de.
The swallow (and I weene it was this Swallowes father) he
Was earliest up, with him I met, and he admired me.
I hild him wing, and wistly he survaies me round about,
And lastly, knowing who I was, did give me many a flout.
And fled to tell the other birds, what uncouth Fowle was bred,
Who flockt to see me, till with gibes and girds I wisht mee ded.
Then, shifting out of sight, I hung till Twilight in a hoole,
Transformde, derided, hunger-spent, and (minding still the
    Moole)
In vaine I wisht reducement of my shape, and (which was
    worste)
My hap was harder than to owne in that distresse a Crust.
Then fled I to my wonted Holes, of hoorded food to get,
Too narrow by mine added wings that did mine entry let.
Now Mise fled me, not to the Moole I would returne for shame,
To *Dis* I durst not, mong'st the Birds I was a laughing game:
Then curst I mine aspiring minde, then knew I *Dis* a Divell,
The Divell the Prince of Pride, and Pride the roote of every
    evill.
Hell, Earth, Aire, Heaven, and what not? then conspiring
    mine unrest,
What might remaine but death for me that lived so unblest?
But as I, fainting, flew that night your Ladiship, Dame Owle,
Did call me to your Todd, and glad to see a new night-fowle,
Did take me to your service, thence your Chamberlaine to be:
Ha *Jupiter* reward it you that so releeved mee.
It is a sweete continuall feast to live content I see:
No daunger but in high estate, none envy meane degree.
    Then all this processe (quoth the Owle) doth tend, belike,
        to this,

That I should eate no Mouse-flesh: Nay, Sir Bat, so sweete it is
That thou, so neere of Kinne to them, shalt also serve my lust:
And therewith in rutheles clawes the haplesse Bat she trust.

The Falcon

IN the *Greek Anthology* there are several poems about the strange deaths of
animals, amongst them the contest of a raven and a scorpion, each of which
kills the other (ix. 339). This epigram was repeatedly made into an emblem
during the sixteenth century: Alciati and Aneau used it. (See James Hutton,
The Greek Anthology in Italy, on versions by Erasmus, Sabeo, and others.)
There were other emblems with the combat of birds such as the heron and
the falcon as their subject. (Camerarius, *Centuriae*, III. xxxii; Jacob Cats,
Alle de wercken, Amsterdam, 1658, p. 542, a stork and a falcon.) Compare
the similes of Ariosto, *Orlando Furioso*, translated by John Harington, xxiv.
79, and Spenser, *Faerie Queene*, VI. vii. 9. Thomas Scot, *Philomythie*, has a
poem, 'Duellum Britannicum', with an emblematic illustration depicting
two falcons killing one another, representing the death at each other's hands
of two of his contemporaries. Lovelace's poem has a particular relationship
to 'Le Vol pour Heron' in Claude Gauchet's *Le Plaisir des Champs* (Paris,
1583), which is closer, however, to the pleasures of the sport, and with the
first chapter of Isaak Walton's *Compleat Angler* (1653), 'The First Day.
A Conference betwixt an *Angler*, a *Falkner* and a *Hunter*, each commending
his Recreation'.

> FAIR Princesse of the spacious Air,
> That hast vouchsaf'd acquaintance here,
> With us are quarter'd below stairs,
> That can reach Heav'n with nought but Pray'rs;[1]
> Who when our activ'st wings we try,
> Advance a foot into the Sky.

> Bright Heir t' th' Bird Imperial,[2]
> From whose avenging penons fall
> Thunder and Lightning twisted Spun;
> Brave Cousin-german to the Sun,[3]

---

[1] Pierius Valerianus, *Hieroglyphica* (Lyons, 1610), 'Accipiter', the falcon symbolizes
pious meditation.

[2] In Walton, the falcon is the eagle's successor as 'Jove's faithful servant in Ordinary'.

[3] Valerianus records that the falcon represented the sun for the Egyptians.

That didst forsake thy Throne and Sphere,
To be a humble Pris'ner here;
And for a pirch of her soft hand,
Resign the Royal Woods command.[1]

How often would'st thou shoot Heav'ns Ark,
Then mount thy self into a Lark;
And after our short faint eyes call,
When now a Fly, now nought at all;[2]
Then stoop so swift unto our Sence,
As thou wert sent Intelligence.[3]

Free beauteous Slave, thy happy feet
In silver Fetters vervails meet,
And trample on that noble Wrist
The Gods have kneel'd in vain t'have kist:
But gaze not, bold deceived Spye,
Too much oth' lustre of her Eye;
The Sun, thou dost out-stare, alas!
Winks at the glory of her Face.[4]

Be safe then in thy Velvet helm,
Her looks are calms that do orewhelm,
Then the *Arabian* bird more blest,
Chafe in the spicery of her breast,
And loose you in her Breath, a wind
Sow'rs the delicious gales of *Inde*.

---

[1] For Valerianus, following Horapollo, the bird is an image of humility in its descent. Cf. Walton, 'I can make her to descend by a word from my mouth (which she both knows and obeyes) to accept of meat from my hand, to own me for her Master'.

[2] *Cymbeline*, I. iii. 14–22: 'Thou should'st have made him | As little as a Crow, or lesse, ere left | To after-eye him . . . | Nay, followed him, till he had melted from | The smalnesse of a Gnat to ayre.' *A Strange Metamorphosis of Man* (1634), xix, 'The Gnat': 'If you take him as he is indeed, is but a point, but an atome, but a little nothing that flies in the aire.'

[3] Milton, *Comus* (1637), 80–81:
> Swift as the Sparkle of a glancing Star,
> I shoot from Heav'n to give him safe convey.

[4] Cf. 'A Lady with a Falcon on her Fist. To the Honourable my Cousin A. L.'

But now a quill from thine own Wing
I pluck, thy lofty fate to sing;
Whilst we behold the various fight,[1]
With mingled pleasure and affright,
The humbler Hinds do fall to pray'r,
As when an Army's seen i' th' Air
And the prophetick Spannels run,
And howle thy *Epicedium*.

The *Heron* mounted doth appear
On his own Peg'sus a Lanceer,
And seems on earth, when he doth hut,
A proper Halberdier on foot;
Secure i' th' Moore, about to sup,[2]
The Dogs have beat his Quarters up.

And now he takes the open air,
Drawes up his Wings with Tactick care;
Whilst th'expert *Falcon* swift doth climbe,
In subtle Mazes serpentine;[3]
And to advantage closely twin'd
She gets the upper Sky and Wind,
Where she dissembles to invade,
And lies a pol'tick Ambuscade.

The hedg'd-in *Heron*, whom the Foe
Awaits above, and Dogs below,[4]
In his fortification lies,
And makes him ready for surprize;
When roused with a shrill alarm,
Was shouted from beneath, they arm.

---

[1] Camerarius, *Centuriae*, III. xxxii, 'Exitus in dubio est.'
[2] Gauchet, 'quelque gourmand heron' is beaten up on the marsh.
[3] Gauchet's falcon 'd'un vigoureax cerceau / Leger tranche le vent'.
[4] Gauchet's heron is also trapped temporarily between falcons and dogs.

The *Falcon* charges at first view
With her bridgade of Talons;[1] through
Whose Shoots, the wary Heron beat,
With a well counter-wheeled retreat.
But the bold Gen'ral never lost,
Hath won again her airy Post;
Who wild in this affront, now fryes,
Then gives a Volley of her Eyes.

The desp'rate *Heron* now contracts,
In one design all former facts;
Noble he is resolv'd to fall
His, and his En'mies funerall,[2]
And (to be rid of her) to dy
A publick Martyr of the Sky.

When now he turns his last to wreak
The palizadoes of his Beak;
The raging foe impatient
Wrack'd with revenge, and fury rent,
Swift as the thunderbolt he strikes,[3]
Too sure upon the stand of Pikes,
There she his naked breast doth hit
And on the case of Rapier's split,

But ev'n in her expiring pangs
The *Heron's* pounc'd within her Phangs,
And so above she stoops to rise
A Trophee and a Sacrifice;[4]
While her own Bells in her sad fall
Ring out the double Funerall.

---

[1] There are suggestions of the military metaphor in Gauchet's 'targue' for a beak and 'pointu comme un daguet'.
[2] Gauchet, 'l'oiseau fort, / Qui dévalle du ceil pour luy donner la mort / Se la donne a luy-mesme.'
[3] Gauchet's falcons resemble thunder in their speed; one is 'furieux'.
[4] Gauchet, 'et leur prise et leur proye'.

Ah Victory, unhap'ly wonne!
Weeping and Red is set the Sunne,
Whilst the whole Field floats in one tear,
And all the Air doth mourning wear:
Close hooded all thy kindred come
To pay their Vows upon thy Tombe;
The *Hobby* and the *Musket* too,
Do march to take their last adieu.

The *Lanner* and the *Lanneret*,
Thy Colours bear as Banneret,
The *Goshawk* and her *Tercel* rows'd,[1]
With Tears attend thee as new bows'd,
All these are in their dark array
Led by the various *Herald-Jay*.[2]

But thy eternal name shall live
Whilst Quills from Ashes fame reprieve,
Whilst open stands Renown's wide dore,
And Wings are left on which to soar;
Doctor *Robbin*, the Prelate *Pye*,
And the poetik *Swan* shall dye,
Only to sing thy Elegie.

The Snayl

THE snail is the subject of Renaissance epigram and mock-heroic, besides
making briefer emblematic or decorative appearances. Rémy Belleau has
his poem 'Le Limaçon', and in an anonymous English poem, *A Herrings
Tale* (1598, reprinted by F. E. Halliday in *Richard Carew of Antony*, 1953),
a snail wages war with a weather-cock. Reusner's *Aenigmatographia* has
several riddles on the snail and its near relation the tortoise.

WISE Emblem of our Politick World,
Sage Snayle, within thine own self curl'd;[3]

---

[1] Walton, 'The *Laner* and *Laneret*', 'The *Goshawk* and *Tarcel*'.
[2] Cf. Claudian, 'Phoenix'; Robert Chester, *Loves Martyr*, 'The Phoenix and the
Turtle'.
[3] The snail is the emblem of self-containedness in Erasmus, *Parabolarum, sive
similium liber* (Strasbourg, 1516), sig. C^v; Camerarius, op. cit. IV. c.

PLATE IV

Joachim Camerarius, *Symbolorum et Emblematum Centuriae* [1st edition],
III, xxxii, Nuremberg, 1590

Instruct me softly to make hast,
Whilst these my Feet go slowly fast.
　　Compendious Snayl! thou seem'st to me,
Large *Euclids* strickt Epitome;[1]
And in each Diagram, dost Fling
Thee from the point unto the Ring.
A Figure now Triangulare,
An Oval now, and now a Square;[2]
And then a Serpentine dost crawl
Now a straight Line, now crook'd, now all.[3]
　　Preventing Rival of the Day,
Th'art up and openest thy Ray,
And ere the Morn cradles the Moon,
Th'art broke into a Beauteous Noon.
Then when the Sun sups in the Deep,
Thy Silver Horns e're *Cinthia's* peep;[4]
And thou from thine own liquid Bed
New *Phoebus* heav'st thy pleasant Head.
　　Who shall a Name for thee create,
Deep Riddle of Mysterious State?
Bold Nature that gives common Birth
To all products of Seas and Earth,
Of thee, as Earth-quakes, is affraid,
Nor will thy dire Deliv'ry aid.
　　Thou thine own daughter then, and Sire,
That Son and Mother art intire,[5]
That big still with thy self dost go,
And liv'st an aged Embrio;

---

[1] Topsell, *The History of Serpents*, 'Of the Spyder': 'Surely *Euclides* that famous *Geometrium* . . . neede not be ashamed to learne from Spyders the drawing of divers of his figures and Geometricall proportions'.
[2] Henry Leuchter in Reusner, *Aenigmatographia*, ed. cit., p. 405, 'Testudine':

　　　　Mira etiam domus est, arguta, oblonga, rotunda,
　　　　Dura, retorta, potens, abdita, clausa, patens.

See also the description of a snail in *A Herrings Tale*.
[3] William Browne, *Britannia's Pastorals*, II. ii. 11-12, 'his many mazes, / Winding meanders and self-knitting traces'.
[4] Lippius in Reusner, p. 338, 'Contrahit exserta parva cornicula fronte'.
[5] Lauterbach in Reusner, p. 8, 'sexu neque mas, neque virgo'.

That like the Cubbs of *India*,[1]
Thou from thy self a while dost play:
But frightened with a Dog or Gun,
In thine own Belly thou dost run.[2]
And as thy house was thine own womb,
So thine own womb, concludes thy tomb.[3]
   But now I must (analys'd King)
Thy Oeconomick Virtues sing;
Thou great stay'd Husband still within,
Thou, thee, that's thine, dost Discipline;[4]
And when thou art to progress bent,
Thou mov'st thy self and tenement,[5]
As Warlike *Scythians* travayl'd, you,
Remove your Men and City too;
Then after a sad Dearth and Rain,
Thou scatterest thy Silver Train;[6]
And when the Trees grow nak'd and old,
Thou cloathest them with Cloth of Gold,
Which from thy Bowels thou dost spin,
And draw from the rich Mines within.
   Now hast thou chang'd thee Saint; and made
Thy self a Fane that's cupula'd;
And in thy wreathed Cloister thou
Walkest thine own Gray fryer too;
Strickt, and lock'd up, th'art Hood all ore
And ne'r Eliminat'st thy Dore.
On Sallads thou dost feed severe,
And 'stead of Beads thou drop'st a tear,
And when to rest, each calls the Bell,
Thou sleep'st within thy Marble Cell;
Where in dark contemplation plac'd,

---

[1] In *A Herrings Tale* it is compared with several animals.
[2] *Love's Labour's Lost*, IV. iii. 335.
[3] *A Herrings Tale*: 'to use his shelly cave / For house, for fort, for clothes, for bed, and for his grave'.
[4] Lauterbach, loc. cit., 'Nunquam non vigilans observo fideliter aedes'.
[5] Reusner, p. 76, *domiporta*.
[6] Hadrianus Junius in Reusner, p. 244, 'quaqua incedo, tractu illino muscum'; Herrick, 'The Temple'; 'Oberon's Palace'.

The sweets of Nature thou doth tast;
Who now with Time thy days resolve,
And in a Jelly thee dissolve.
Like a shot Star, which doth repair
Upward, and Rarifie the Air.

I

The Ladie Emilia saide: we shall now trye your wit. And if all
be true I have hearde, there have beene men so wittie and eloquent,
that they have not wanted matter to make a booke in the prayse
of a flie.[1]

. . . we cannot but thinke that every story of a beast is like a
severall Hymne, to praise the Divine wisdome and goodnes, from
which as from a pure, ever-springing fountaine, proceed and flow
all good, beautifull and wise actions.[2]

These words, taken from two books well known around 1600,
represent two poles in the poetry of the sixteenth and seventeenth centuries which is concerned with small creatures. They
might provoke humorous hyperbole or reverence, or provide
occasion for minute description. Yet there was no neat separation of the comic from the didactic; wit and piety were combined in a way that affronts a stricter decorum.

Wonder was the frame of mind affiliating such discords, a
wonder compounded of religious awe and the capacity for
being surprised, an acceptance of the world both as the
Creator's joke and as His riddle, veiling and yet revealing
divine truth. It was the early Fathers of the Church who in
their meditations on the creatures had smoothed out distinc-
tions between small and great in their adoration of the Maker
of all things.

Tell me which is more straunge, the teeth of the Bore, or of the
Moath, the winges of the Griffin, or of the Gnat: the head of the

---

[1] Castiglione, *The Courtier*, translated by Sir Thomas Hoby (1561), Everyman ed.,
p. 105.
[2] Edward Topsell, *The Historie of Four-Footed Beastes* (1607), sig. ¶3ᵛ, 'The First
Epistle of Conradus Gesnerus'.

Horse, or of the Grasse-hopper: The thigh of an Elephaunt, or of a Flye: The snowte of a Sow, or the beake of a Wrenne: An Eagle, or an Ante: A Lyon, or a Gnat: A Tiger or a Snayle.[1]

Augustine had drawn attention to such marvels as the changing colours of the sea, 'the barkes of trees, and skinnes of beasts', and had reflected that 'the fabrike of the Bee or Pismier is more admired then the Whales'.[2] Hugh of St. Victor expanded on the same sentiments:

A little body made with great wysedome. Great wisdom in the which there is no oversight, but hath geven them eyes, which the eye can scantely spye, and in so little bodyes, all the partes be so fitly, & fully fynished, that there wanteth nothing in the least of all the same thinges, wherewith nature hath bewtified the greatest.[3]

Within Hugh's *De operibus trium dierum* is presented a rudimentary measure for the enjoyment of the natural world. The beauty of the creatures lies in their order, movement and growth, in their shape and colour and in their appeal to the other senses. A harmony among these satisfies the whole personality of man in an act of contemplation, 'insomuch that amazed and mervayling, we crye oute with good king David: How marvaylous are thy workes, O Lorde'.[4] The aspects of the creatures which cause enjoyment are not only beauty of form and patterned detail, but the extraordinary and the grotesque, through which truth also comes.

For there be foure things, that therefore men the rather wonder at, because they see them seldom, eyther because there be fewe of

----

[1] Hugh of St. Victor, *De vanitate mundi*, vii (*Patr. Lat.* clxxvi), translated by Richard Coortesse, Bishop of Chichester, as *A Treatise of the Workes of Three Dayes* (1577), sig. Ei^r; also by Thomas Heywood, *The Hierarchie*. See also Pliny, *Historia naturalis*, XI. ii, and Edward Benlowes, *Theophila* (1652), XII. lxxiv:

More than at Tusks of Bores we wonder at
This *Moths* strange Teeth! Legs of this *Gnat*
Pass large-limm'd Gryphons; Then on *Bees* we musing sat;

[2] *St. Augustine, of the Citie of God*, ed. cit., XXII. xxiv. 909.
[3] Coortesse, op. cit., sig. Ei^r.
[4] Ibid., sig. Biv^r.

the kind, or else because they be farre of, or hid in the secrete places of nature, which the wisedome of the maker setteth alone . . . that the slownes of man should be quickned with the novelty of such as be strange to consider the wisedome of God.[1]

Aristotle, too, before the Fathers, had given authority for this kind of outlook, as Bacon and Henry Peacham the younger each recognized in his fashion. As *The Advancement of Learning* has it, '*Aristotle* noteth well, *that the nature of every thing is best seene in his smallest portions*'.[2] For Peacham, in *Graphice* (1612), his manual on the art of painting, God is the artist who 'giveth us to admire that excellent wisdom of his in distinguishing so many beautifull colours from the wings of the proud Peacocks and Ostrich, even unto the poore Butterflie, so that astonished with *Aristotle*, I may say even in those little painted creatures, there is some wonder or other, and in the very border of their wings an evident taste of the divine omnipotence'.[3]

These sentiments were the basis of certain special interests among painters and natural historians of the seventeenth century, especially the exquisite paintings of *minutiae* and the microscopic observations of the new scientists. Though the main treatises on the microscope in England were Henry Power's *Experimental Philosophy* (1664) and Robert Hooke's *Micrographia* (1665), the instrument had been in use, both in Europe and in England, much earlier.[4] In accounts of such work there appears the repeated suggestion that the kind of vision previously accessible only to the devout mind or to the poetic imagination was now accessible to every man through

[1] Coortesse, op. cit., sig. Ei[r].

[2] From Aristotle, *Politics*, I. iii. I, *The Advancement of Learning*, ed. cit. Book II, fol. 9[v]. See also *De partibus animalium* 645[a]17, translated by Gesner, see *The Historie of Four-Footed Beastes*, sig. ¶3[v].

[3] P. 2.

[4] See *Novum Organum* (1620), II. xxxix; John Tradescant, *Musaeum Tradescantianum* (1656), p. 43, 'Severall sorts of Magnifying glasses'. Samuel Hartlib's diary, the *Ephemerides*, for 1635, records the use of one at Kynaston's academy. Miss Marjorie Nicholson's *The Microscope and English Imagination* (Smith College, 1935), a valuable pioneer study, is vitiated by the opinion that a new conception of God and man followed upon microscopic studies.

the microscope. So the early Fathers were right in their intui-
tions, more accurate than their eyesight could confirm.

> This to our minde th' a'theriall wisdome bringes
> how God is greatest in the Least of things
> And in the smallest print wee gather hence
> the world may Best reade his omnipotence.
> Goe on Dioptrick Artist's still goe on
> may your glass-eyes even Vie perfection
> With natures Noblest sense: from yow wee hope
> such rare Emprovements of the Microscope
> That the Magnetick fluors of the stone
> Shall bee as cleerely Seene as now there's none.
> Nay then yow pretty sprit's & fairy Elves
> that hover in the aire Looke to your selves.
> For with such prying Spectacles as these
> Wee shall see yow in your own essences.
> Then shall I see a Soule just when tis gone
> As cleere as now I doe our will: & John.[1]

There are several strands to the interest in small creatures;
and one is a belief in the importance of the commonplace:

> . . . behold the difference of trees, plants, hearbs, and flowers,
> which in each Countrey groweth, with such diversity of colour,
> taste, smell, propertie, and vertue: and these thinges, because we
> see them daily with our eyes, and handle them with our hands as
> thinges common, doe not amaze us, why should wee then so much
> wonder in seeing some things which passe this common agreement
> and order of nature?[2]

This attitude had its two-way movement, either to a religious
interpretation of the universe, in which all creatures are sacred,
or to a scientific reverence for 'familiar and frequent objects',
the study of which is 'carelessly admitted, and their causes never
inquired after'. Nor were the religious and the scientific
mutually exclusive. A scientist like Robert Boyle could see
a resemblance, if not an identification, between the minute

---

[1] Henry Power, 'Microscopicall observations (1661). In Comendation of ye Microscope' (British Museum, Sloane MS. 1380, art. 16), printed *Isis*, xxi, no. 60 (1934).
[2] Antonio de Torquemada, *The Spanish Mandevile of Miracles* (1600), fol. 3.

attention given to things by the contemplative and by the user of the microscope.[1]

A second feature of this interest in small creatures was the high value placed upon fine craftsmanship, in both nature and art, even to the point of excess. This is clearly stated in Gesner's epistle which prefaced Topsell's *Historie of Four-Footed Beastes*: 'for all workemen do shew more art, skill, and cunning in the small and little price of worke, then the greater'.[2] So there is something particularly remarkable about ants made from ivory and golden fleas, as well as Alexander's Iliads in a nutshell. Robert Hooke, in his *Micrographia*, had much to say about nature's 'curiosity' as well as about the 'useful informations' to be got from minute studies. The word 'curiosity' had acquired several senses since its introduction during the fourteenth century with the meaning 'careful workmanship'. For the Elizabethans it might mean vain speculation or frivolous over-elaboration; but it was also gathering to itself the related senses of ingenuity, connoisseurship, carefulness of construction, and strangeness. By Hooke it was used especially with the sense of mathematical precision ('the Points of the most curious Mathematical Instruments'), of elaborate craftsmanship ('you can hardly look on the scales of any Fish, but you may discover abundance of curiosity and beautifying'), of delicacy ('the finest Lawn . . . so curious that the threads were scarce discernable by the naked eye'), and of surprising novelty ('an infinite variety of curiously figur'd *Snow*').[3] In texture and shape and varied colouring nature appeared to be as intricate and finicking as the most precise contemporary craftsman, if not more so, and was called in to justify excitement at the extremes of elaboration.

[1] Op. cit., p. 30.   [2] Sig. ¶2ᵛ.
[3] *Micrographia* (1665), pp. 2, 163, 5, 91. Cf. Herrick, *Hesperides*, no. 294 (ed. cit., p. 119):

> Shapcot: To thee the Fairy State
> I with discretion, dedicate.
> Because thou prizest things that are
> Curious, and un-familiar.

John Wilkins, *The Beauty of Providence*, p. 57, renders the Greek of *Ephesians* iii. 10 as 'Interchangeable wisedom, of curious variety'.

Nature is curious, and such *worke* may shape
That our dull *sense* can never finde, but scape.[1]

If Natures skill in optick's yow would trye
then take a Flea & looke mee at her eye.
Where in an Emarauld Iris shee hath sett,
(empaled with white) a pupill all of jett.
Change but your object Looke at common flyes
How their soules peepe through Lattices of eyes.

.   .   .   .   .

Here are the Curious Mathematick's Here
lyes the rare skill of their Artificeere.
All things hee made of nothing, but in this
hee made a thinge that lesse then Nothing is.[2]

The third important feature of this interest in small creatures
is the making of comparisons with the normal world. It was
the traditional manner of expressing surprise at nature's ingenuities. Pliny had done it, and then St. Augustine; and the
theologians and scientists of our period followed suit. We can
find it in Petrus Borellus's *Observationum Microscopicarum Cen-
turia* (1656),[3] whose character-sketches of insects were imitated
by the English microscopists. The tiniest creatures are changed
to the dimensions of a Colossus through the instrument, a
spider resembles a bear, a flea a prawn, sand jewels, and a fly
an elephant, in support of the ancient proverb, *de musca elephan-
tum facere.*[4] Henry Power and Robert Hooke were not averse
to analogies of the same kind, between a seed of thyme and 'a
dish of Lemmons' 'plac'd in a very little Room', between the
gnat and the rhinoceros, the water-gnat and the ox. This kind
of comparison is obviously close to the hyperboles of the
mock-heroic style: it was a proof that nature itself was witty.
There was, however, another kind of analogy-making, connected with the fact that the Creator had put a soul within so

---

[1] Margaret Cavendish, Duchess of Newcastle, *Poems and Fancies* (1653), p. 44, 'Of
many Worlds in this World'.
[2] From Henry Power, 'Microscopicall observations'.
[3] Published as part of *De vero Telescopii Inventore, cum brevi omnium conspiciliorum
historia* (The Hague, 1655–6).
[4] See Tilley, *A Dictionary of Proverbs*, F. 398, from Erasmus, *Adagia*.

tiny a body.[1] If in physiological structure an insect could resemble the larger creatures, it might also mirror some aspect of divine truth in small space. This is the sense in which the smallest shows forth the greatest in microscopical investigations for Theodore Mayerne in his preface to Thomas Moufet's book, *The Theater of Insects* (1658). (Its Latin version, *Theatrum Insectorum*, had appeared in 1634.) And there was more than a slight connexion between the emblem, an insignificant pictorial body containing a soul of important meaning, and the symbolic significance given to so many of the tiny creatures. The end of that kind of analogy-making was not amusement but awe, the surprise not of laughter but of wonder. Only the two frequently met.[2]

II

Poems concerning small creatures had a varied ancestry. A miscellany of continental and English poems of a hexaemeral or enumerative sort have affiliations with the encyclopaedias of natural history, though their writers might have claimed for them some classical model.[3] Du Bartas's successive prefaces to his *Deux Semaines* from 1578 onwards tell their own tale; for at first he professed to be writing an imitation of classical epic, of Homer, Virgil, and Ariosto, whereas by 1584 he was

[1] Augustine on small creatures (see p. 82) was quoted by Theodore Gaza in a commentary on Aristotle's *De partibus animalium*, and by Topsell, op. cit., sig. A5^r.

[2] See E. R. Curtius, *European Literature and the Latin Middle Ages* (1953), Excursus iv, 'Jest and Earnest in Medieval Literature'; H. K. Miller, 'The Paradoxical Encomium with special reference to its Vogue in England, 1600–1800', *M.P.* (1956), 145–78.

[3] In Latin, examples are George Buchanan, *Sphera* (1585); Adam King, *De theoria planetarum* (1616); David Kinloch, *De hominis procreatione* (1596); Abraham Cowley, *De plantis* (1662). See Leicester Bradner, *Musae Anglicanae* (Baltimore, 1940). In English, examples are Thomas Moufet, *The Silkewormes and their Flies* (1599); Robert Chester, *Love's Martyr* (1601), celebrating England's riches and God's bounty, with a herbal, a bestiary, and a lapidary; Sir John Beaumont, *The Metamorphosis of Tabacco* [1602]; Nathaniel Baxter, *Sir Philip Sydney's Ourania, That is, Endimion's Song and Tragedie, containing all Philosophie* (1606); Michael Drayton, *Poly-Olbion* (1612, 1622) and *Noah's Floud* (1630); John Taylor, *The Praise of Hempseed* (1620); John Hagthorpe, *Visiones Rerum* (1623); Phineas Fletcher, *The Purple Island* (1633); Thomas Nabbes, *Microcosmus* (1637); Margaret Cavendish, *Poems and Fancies* (1653); Nicholas Billingsley, Κοσμοβρεφια or the *Infancy of the World* (1658); Samuel Pordage, *Mundorum Explicatio* (1661); Barten Holyday, *A Survey of the World* (1661).

describing his poem as a compendium reflecting the varieties of nature, 'toutes sciences et professions', 'une infinité de points de mathématiques, métaphysique, médicine, et théologie scholastique', 'la nature de toutes les choses qui sont au monde'.[1] His real models were not Lucretius and the *Georgics*, but rather the cosmological myths and hymns of Péletier le Mans and Ronsard, as well as a mass of other verse less accomplished, though often lengthy and generally encyclopaedic in tone.[2]

There were those critical extremists who denied the name of poetry to any kind of natural philosophy in verse, even the *Georgics*,[3] on the grounds that there was no thematic invention in such poems, but a close adherence to existent things rather than to the imaginary, and a tendency to graceless triviality, technicality, and an unselective minuteness of detail. On the other hand, learned poetry had its defenders in plenty,[4] and British readers agreed in their admiration of it, as the popularity of the poems of Palingenius and of Du Bartas signifies.[5] Even so, knowledge tended to appear rather under the disguise of allegory and Ovidian tale of metamorphosis, or as part of a hymn, in a narrative of creation, or in simile and metaphor. Landscape is transformed into pageant, anatomy is allegorized, natural events and objects are given fanciful explanations, and if learning appears in these unscientific tales, it is to give an additional bite to the entertainment.

The extended poem on small creatures was particularly

---

[1] *The Works of Guillaume De Saluste Sieur Du Bartas*, ed. U. T. Holmes, J. C. Lyons, R. W. Linker (Chapel Hill: University of North Carolina Press, 1935–40), i, Appendix D.

[2] See Albert-Marie Schmidt, *La Poésie Scientifique en France au Seizième Siècle* (Paris, 1938); V. Zabughin, *Virgilio nel Rinascimento Italiano* (Bologna, 1921).

[3] See Minturno, *De poeta . . . libri sex* (Venice, 1559), pp. 26, 30; L. Castelvetro, *La Poetica d'Aristotele volgarizza* (Venice, 1570), in A. H. Gilbert, *Literary Criticism: Plato to Dryden* (New York, 1940), p. 307.

[4] See Frances Yates, *The French Academies of the Sixteenth Century* (1947), v; J. C. Scaliger, *Poetices Libri VII* (Lyons, 1561), I. ii, III. xxvi, v. iii; William Webbe, *A Discourse of English Poetrie* (1586), in Gregory Smith, *Elizabethan Critical Essays* (1904), i. 236; *Gabriel Harvey's Marginalia*, ed. G. C. Moore-Smith (Stratford-upon-Avon, 1913), p. 159.

[5] *S.T.C.* lists nine Latin editions of Palingenius in England, 1572–1639, and five editions of Googe's translation, part or whole, 1560–87; and twenty editions of Du Bartas in translation, part or whole, by various hands, 1595–1625.

associated with the literary habit of hyperbolic expansion and dilation upon trivialities.[1] The merits of such writing were not unconnected with its length, the *tour de force* involved in keeping something up for as long as possible, matching style with the extent of laughter or reverence. This was to 'Make of the flie, an Elephant, and of a matter of nothing, a long tale'.[2] This kind of expansion could work in two directions, either towards meticulous telling of the truth about a creature, or towards sustained deception and metamorphosis, the prolongation of a lie, in order to amuse; yet these two approaches might be combined. For Minturno, the poet who described the natural world convincingly was the greater deceiver and the more skilful because of it;[3] for Thomas May, translating the *Georgics* in 1628, to write well of comparative trivialities was a test both of the ingenuity of the poet and of the elasticity of the language ('How full of heights not improperly raised out of a meane subject').[4] The Virgilian phrases *in tenui labor; at tenuis non gloria* and *si parva licet componere magnis*[5] became the *credo* of many poets treating commonplace subjects, and the *Georgics* themselves were probably read with expectations not entirely different from those brought to the poetic paradox. When a more important reason than entertainment was given for the magnification of small creatures, it was usually in terms of their significance as examples for human society (this is how Puttenham defends the Homeric *Batrachomyomachia*),[6] or as emblems containing elevated thoughts in a humble body. This is Robert Boyle's defence of a '*Subtil*' and a '*Magnificent*' style.

. . . oftentimes, when the *Protasis*, or former part of a Reflection, is spent upon considering some mean and Trival subject; the *Apodosis*, or Reddition, contains such an Application of what one was taking notice of in the Subject, that the thing Pointed at, may be

[1] See the article by H. K. Miller already cited, and A. S. Pease, 'Things without Honor', *Classical Philology*, xxi (1926), 27–42, for classical background.
[2] See Tilley, op. cit., F. 398, from Pettie, *Civile Conversation* (1581).
[3] *De poeta libri sex* (Venice, 1559), p. 31.
[4] *Virgils Georgicks* (1628), preface.
[5] *Georgics*, iv. 6, and 176.
[6] *The Arte of English Poesie*, III. v, 'Of Stile'.

some important Moral Instruction, or perhaps some Theological Mystery.[1]

Virgil's ants and bees were the models for a manner noble and vivid, for 'some lively and apt description, dress'd in such colours of speech, that it sets before your eyes the absent object, as perfectly and more delightfully than nature'.[2] When that was written, the praise of trivialities was giving way to the picturesque style, and the element of paradox and playful hyperbole, never very far away in Renaissance poems about things without honour, was being subdued for the sake of a more decorous manner. Yet even the new criteria might be used to defend old habits. An example of this is Robert Wolseley's defence of Rochester's poems by an appeal to a standard of true wit which is 'to make a very little Picture of anything that really exists', drawing support from Virgil's 'Descriptions of the Employment of Bees, the Jealousie of Bulls, the Lust of Horses and Boars, the cutting down of a Tree, the Working of Ants, and the Swimming and Hissing of Snakes, things little and unlovely in themselves, but noble and beautiful in the Picture he gives us of 'em'.[3] The poet may idealize the real; he may also make paradoxical praise of what is unpraiseworthy. For Horace has said of Homer that he 'can fetch Light out of Smoak, Roses out of Dunghils, and give a kind of Life to the Inanimate'.

For the growth of interest in the writing of short poems on insect, animal, or plant, 1494, the year of the first printing of the *Greek Anthology*,[4] and 1554, the year of the printing of Henri Estienne's edition of Anacreon,[5] are important dates. Of course, only a relatively small number of these classical epigrams and lyrics dealt particularly with the creatures, but these shared their popularity with poems more distinctly amatory

---

[1] Boyle, *Occasional Reflections* (ed. cit.), 'An Introductory Preface', sig. a6ᵛ.

[2] Dryden, preface to 'Annus Mirabilis' (1666).

[3] 'Preface to Valentinian' (1685), in Spingarn, *Critical Essays of the Seventeenth Century* (1908), iii. 15–16.

[4] See James Hutton, *The Greek Anthology in France and the Latin Writers of the Netherlands to the Year 1800* (Cornell University Press, 1946).

[5] See Henri Chamard, *Historie de la Pléiade* (Paris, 1939), II. xiii, 'L'Anacréontisme de Ronsard'.

or didactic. So the taste was accentuated for pleasing trivialities, *folastries*, in which craftsmanship in small space and refinement on a tradition of associations are all-important.

The brief *lusus*, like the paradoxical encomium, had a new lease of life during the sixteenth century as a relaxation for the learned and the polite. This kind of poem, with its own relation to the classical epigram, seems to have been developed during the Middle Ages, and was revived in Italy by Berni, in the tradition of the *strambottisti*. From them Marot learned to write his paradoxical praises, and from Marot Ronsard. With the *Pléiade* came the juncture of several kinds in the vernacular, a coalescence of native tradition with a rediscovery of the classical epigram. Short odes, *strambotti*, epigrams, and blasons, Ronsard united all these different kinds to make poems in which the descriptive element and the humorous are usually associated. Yet the brief poem need not be simply amusing: it might be reflective, with emblematic under-tones. 'Jesters do oft prove prophets.'

The fairy-poetry which is a special expression of an interest in minuteness seems to have an indefinite yet recognizable connexion both with the mock-heroic[1] and with the epigram.[2] One of the most notable characteristics of this small world is that elves and insects fraternize freely.

The justification of brevity as an estimable quality in poetry was not unrelated to a more general admiration of smallness. Ben Jonson combined literary judgement with the praise of a short life in his poem, 'To the immortall memorie, and friendship of that noble paire, Sir Lucius Cary and Sir H. Morison':

> In small proportions, we just beautie see:
> And in short measures, life may perfect bee.[3]

---

[1] See, for example, William Browne, *Britannia's Pastorals*, iii.

[2] See *Greek Anthology*, xi. 88–95 and 99–111, where small men are compared to insects and other small objects, and Martial, xi. 18, 'In Lupum', translated Cartwright, 1651. M. W. Latham, *The Elizabethan Fairies* (New York, 1930), does not consider this literary tradition.

[3] *Ben Jonson*, ed. Herford and Simpson (Clarendon Press, Oxford, 1925), viii. 245, associated in the commentary with Seneca, *Epistles*, xciii. 7.

'Measures' is carried over from the previous stanza, 'The
Stand', in which aesthetic and moral values are again compared.

> her measures are, how well
> Each syllab'e answer'd, and was form'd, how faire;
> These make the lines of life, and that's her ayre.

Jonson was not the only seventeenth-century poet to play on
the multiple meanings of words like 'measures' and 'lines'.
Fanshawe rendered Horace's *fines* by 'lines'.

> There is a mean in things, and certain lines
> Within which virtue still itself confines.[1]

Brevity might mean pith and neatness, or it might mean a
concentration of wit, the 'Enucleate Mysteries' of metaphor,[2]
and the compressed significance of the emblem.

> Th'Philosophers *Elixir* in each line
> Doth in Epitome all that's rich confine.[3]

When Cowley wrote of the '*Great Wit*' which 'is no more tyed
to live in a *vast Volume*, then in a *Gigantick Body*', but which is
on the contrary 'more vigorous the less space it animates',[4] it
is difficult to distinguish the brevity of concise and pertinent
statement from the brevity of figurative analogy. It is likely
that his poetic ideal, shared with many contemporaries, was
not untouched by the desire to approach the condition of the
epigram.

> *Long Poetry* some cannot bee friends withall: and indeed, it palles
> upon the reading. The wittiest *Poets* have beene all *short*, and chang-
> ing soone their *Subject*; as Horace, Martiall, Juvenall, Seneca, and the

---

[1] *Satires*, I. i. 106–7, in Horace's *Poems* (ed. for H. Brome, 1666), p. 1067.
[2] Benlowes, 'To my Fancie upon Theophila'.
[3] John Collop, *Poesis Rediviva* (1656), pp. 1–2, 'The Poet'.
[4] Preface to *Poems* (1656). He quotes Statius's lines on little Tydaeus,

> Totos infusa per artus
> Major in exiguo regnabat corpore virtus.

Cf. Michael Mayer, *Lusus Serius: Or, Serious Passe-time. A Philosophicall Discourse concerning the Superiority of Creatures under Man* (1654), translated by J. de la Salle, p. 46,
on Tydaeus: 'a very little man, but of a vast and *Gigantick* spirit, For vertue inclos'd
in a narrow roome becomes stronger by compression.'

two *Comoedians*. *Poetry* should be rather like a *Coranto*, *short*, and *nimbly-lofty*; than a *dull Lesson*, of a day long.[1]

Later, Rapin was to separate that 'neatness', not facetious but sweet, 'mean and unsurprizing', from the point and pun in small space, as good from bad;[2] but, for weal or for woe, these two sorts of brevity stayed together in much of the most characteristic poetry of the seventeenth century.

In his poem, 'Upon Appleton House', Marvell was to add to the analogy between life and art in terms of 'lines'.

> *Humility* alone designs
> Those short but admirable Lines,
> By which, ungirt and unconstrain'd,
> Things greater are in less contain'd.[3]

The 'Lines' have become the boundaries of the virtuous man's house, calling in recollections of a familiar pastoral idea, which was stated in the 'Proemio' of Sannazzaro's *Arcadia* (1504): 'Che certo egli e migliore il poco terreno ben coltivare, che'l molto lasciare per mal governo miseramente imboschire.'[4] The terminology of literary criticism mingled easily with the terminology of stoicism and of patristic asceticism and devotion.

The association which existed between small poems and small creatures cannot be better demonstrated than by a poem called 'The Insect. against Bulk. *Inest sua gratia parvis*. by Mr. Yalden'.[5] The concentration of perfection 'in a small space' is compared with the contraction of beams in a burning-glass, with the imitation of great by small in Archimedes's sphere.

> Wher Greatness is to Nature's Works deny'd,
> In *Worth* and *Beauty* it is well supply'd:
> In a small space the more Perfection's shown,
> And what is exquisite, in Little's done.

---

[1] Owen Feltham, *Resolves or Excogitations. A Second Centurie* (1628), p. 202, 'Of Poets and Poetrie'.

[2] Rapin, 'De Carmine Pastorali', translated Thomas Creech (Oxford, 1684).

[3] *Poems and Letters*, ed. H. M. Margoliouth (Clarendon Press, Oxford, 1952), ii. 60.

[4] Cf. the aphorisms quoted in J. Camerarius, *De Re Rustica* (Nuremberg, 1596); p. 25: 'Foecundior est culta exiguitas, quam magnitudo neglecta' (Palladius); 'Laudato ingentia rura, Exiguum colito' (Virgil); and p. 117: 'Exiguus spacio, variis sed fertilis herbis'.

[5] *Examen Poeticum* (1693), iii. 370–2.

Thus *Beams* contracted in a narrow Glass,
To Flames convert their larger useless Rays.

The old idea that nature's monsters are less acceptable than her
minutiae ('No Labour can she boast more wonderful, / Than
to inform an *Atom* with a Soul') sits comfortably alongside the
newer distinction between the graceful and the sublime (which
alone it is appropriate to 'admire'). What is most interesting to
our purposes, however, is the literary analogy, and the changing
conception of the epigram which it suggests, the shift from
emblematic fullness to correctness.

Thus does the little Epigram delight,
And charm us with its miniature of Wit:
Whilst tedious *Authors* give the Reader pain,
Weary his thoughts, and make him toil in vain;
When in less Volume we more pleasure find
And what diverts, still best informs the Mind.

'Tis the small Insect looks correct and fair,
And seems the product of her nicest Care.
. . .
Then she the Insect frames, her Masterpiece,
Made for Diversion, and design'd to please.
. . .
Then since the least so beautifully show,
B' advised in time, my Muse, and learn to know
A Poet's lines shou'd be correct, and few.

III

It became a literary habit to introduce one's own work in
praise of trivialities with a list of precedents,[1] and the Virgilian
poem, *Culex*, commonly appeared amongst them. For John
Taylor, in his preamble to *The Praise of Hempseed* (1620), it
was the element of *tour de force* which was the important

---

[1] See Statius's epistle to Stella (the preface to *Silvae*, i), which refers to *Culex* and
Bachatromyomachia; Erasmus, *The Praise of Folly*; Gabriel Harvey, *Pierces Supererogation*
(1593); *Nashes Lenten Stuffe* (1599); Michael Drayton, *The Owle* (1619), which
mentions *Culex*, *Bachatromyomachia*, and Vida's *De Bombyce*.

quality common to the works he mentioned. Mock-heroic and epigram, allegory and pastoral, Ovidian narrative and prose instruction, courtly complimentary lyric and satire are grouped together by virtue of sharing one characteristic, that they are in praise of 'unpoetic' subjects. Thomas Scot, on the other hand, in his *Philomythie* (1616), compared Aesop, *Culex*, Spenser's *Mother Hubberds Tale*, and Phineas Fletcher's *Locustae* with his own poems, because they also had been criticized for hiding political references within fables. Introducing his own version of the Virgilian poem, Spenser himself described it as not only 'a jest' but also a 'riddle rare' of his own experience, a combination which his interpreters have not always appreciated.[1] It was still another quality common to several poems on small creatures, including '*Virgils Gnat*', '*Marshals Bee*', Vida's silkworm, and his own 'rare *Phil*, that lately was / With Lillies Tomb'd up in a Glasse'[2] which Herrick selected in his epitaph on a fly[3]—the enclosure of beauty in small space. If the same poem, *Culex*, could be regarded as a joke, as a political allegory, and as the praise of a beautiful creature, this is some indication of the levels at which it could be read, none excluding the other. Wit and wonder had met together, and their embrace was the discovery of truth.

An easy conjunction of solemnity and humour is in evidence in the longer narrative poems concerned with the creatures which appeared during our period. Folk-tale and the imitation of the *Metamorphoses* coalesce in the explanatory sort of genealogical myth.[4] A variation on this kind of narrative is the topographical tale,[5] introduced into England by Camden,

---

[1] 'Virgils Gnat' (1591), 'Dedicatory Sonnet'. See the *Variorum Spenser*, ii, 'Minor Poems'.

[2] *Hesperides*, no. 257, 'Upon the death of his Sparrow. An Elegie' (ed. cit., p. 103).

[3] Ibid., no. 498 (ed. cit., p. 185).

[4] J. C. Scaliger, *Poetices*, III. cxvi, interpreted classical mythical genealogies in terms of natural history, and approved of their contemporary use in that sense. English examples are Spenser, *Muiopotmos* (1590); William Warner, *Albions England*, VII. xxxvii; Richard Carew, *A Herrings Tale* (1598); Sir John Beaumont, *The Metamorphosis of Tabacco* (1602); Thomas Moufet, *The Silkewormes and their Flies* (1599); Robert Herrick, *Hesperides* (1648).

[5] See Rudolf Gottfried, 'Spenser and the Italian Myth of Locality', *S.P.* xxxiv (1937), 107–25.

popularized by Spenser,[1] and imitated by Michael Drayton throughout *Poly-Olbion*, and by William Browne. These poems might be intended as pure entertainment, giving an heroic origin to something of no importance (this is the tone adopted by Carew and Beaumont in accounting for the snail and the tobacco-plant) or concentrating upon delicate detail, elaborated in the manner of *Muiopotmos*, or kept brief in Herrick's manner. Sometimes the moral tone is strong; sometimes the poem is a courtly compliment to the person who caused a metamorphosis, or the patriotic praise of a favourite place.

The mock-heroic battle is another narrative-device which might be the vehicle for religious or political allegory,[2] or for light-hearted description.[3] Readers of Du Bartas would have found there several animal-battles,[4] which set the style until it was succeeded by the somewhat contrived Virgilian phrases of poems like Edmund Waller's 'The Battell of the Summer Islands' (1645).[5]

The traditional animal tale included within its scope a number of other kinds of narrative, which are well represented in Thomas Scot's *Philomythie*,[6] a collection less genial than Aesop, though acknowledging his example, taking a moral standpoint, cautious, anti-Papist, upholding order. Scot's creatures might be grotesque, drawn from Isidore, yet to the discerning they would suggest contemporary situations, since nature 'Mixt us in common with th'Antipodes'.[7] The deception,[8] and its corollary the mistaken allegiance (the leading patterns in *Mother Hubberds Tale*), appear in Scot's stories of the dogs which follow the king's hunt and are consumed by a crocodile (the

[1] See *Faerie Queene*, VII. vi. 40–55; IV. xi. 8–53; *Colin Clout's Come Home Again*, 104–65.

[2] John Heywood, *The Spider and the Flie* (1556); Phineas Fletcher, *The Locusts* (1627).

[3] Such as Richard Carew, op. cit., and Richard Lovelace, 'The Falcon' and 'The Toad and Spider' (1660).

[4] See, for examples, 'The Sixt Day of the First Week'.

[5] Other hunting-poems are Sir Robert Howard, *The Duell of the Stags* (1668) (Cf. *Poly-Olbion*, xiii. 87–161); Denham, *Cooper's Hill* (1642, 1655).

[6] There were two editions in 1616, two in 1622, and one in 1625.

[7] Sig. B^v.

[8] Cf. Richard Niccols, *The Beggers Ape* (1627).

second tale, 'Venaticum Iter'), of the hyena which deceives the
ass and the musk-cat (the fourth tale, 'Sphinx, Hyena'), of the
chameleon and the polypus which are tricksters (the fifth tale,
'Hippopotamus'), and of the water-pirate cormorant whose
protection is worse than enmity (the eighth tale, 'Onocratalus').
The marriage is represented by the sixth tale, 'Phoenix',[1] and
the fall of the aspirant by the eleventh, 'Curiale', which con-
cerns a fly and a flea at the royal court. In Scot's fabulous world,
the amphibian has its special satirical function, as an image of
the equivocator, the double-minded man. (The griffin in
'Gryps', the third tale, the lamprey in 'Unio', the seventh, and
the cormorant in the eighth are of this kind.)

The debate, which is obviously the most popular scheme of
organization among animal-narratives, is represented in *Philomythie* by the seventh tale, in which the mole, the lamprey,
the chameleon, and the salamander argue about the virtues of
the four elements to which they belong;[2] and by the third, in
which the griffin offers itself as king of the creatures because it
is both bird and beast, but is rejected by man. Sometimes a
group of creatures come to pay court or to give judgement on
a cause:[3] Sidney's poem 'As I my little flocke on *Ister* banke'[4]
and George Herbert's 'Humilitie'[5] are of this kind. Sometimes
two or more are in conversation or opposition: in *The Cuckow*
(1607) by Richard Niccols, the birds choose the cuckoo rather
than the nightingale as the patron of love, in *Democritus his
Dreame* (1605) by Peter Woodhouse, the elephant and the flea
debate about modesty and pride,[6] in *The Ant and the Nightingale,
or Father Hubberds Tales* (1604), attributed to Thomas Middleton,

---

[1] Cf. Robert Chester, *Love's Martyr* (1600); 'Thomas Cutwode', *Caltha Poetarum*
(1599).

[2] Other contests among the elements are Drayton, *Muses Elizium*, 'Sixt Nimphall',
Anne Bradstreet, *The Tenth Muse* (1650), Margaret Cavendish, *Poems and Fancies*
(1653), and in prose Izaak Walton, *The Compleat Angler* (1653), 'The First Day'.

[3] For prose-allegories of the 'parliament' type see James Howell, *Dodona's Grove*
(1644); Michael Mayer, *Lusus Serius* (1654); and in Latin verse, see Cowley, *De
Plantis*, iii–vi.

[4] *Arcadia*, ed. cit., pp. 132–7.

[5] *The Works*, ed. F. E. Hutchinson (1941), p. 70.

[6] See also Samuel Wesley, *Maggots* (1685), 'A Dialogue Between the Herring and
the Whale'.

the ant tells its life-story, in a mixture of prose and verse. Sometimes one creature brings its case against others for the preservation of society: Lady Nature defends her favourite, the phoenix, in *Loves Martyr* (1600). In *The Owle* (1604, 1619) by Drayton, the bird of that name flies by night, observing injustice and corruption at all levels of society, and places its case before King Eagle, warning the bird-kingdom of the dangerous position of their perching-place.[1] Samuel Rowland's satire, *The Night-Raven* (1620), has a similar bird, observant of the vices of the city. But perhaps the most entertaining of these poems of dialogue and debate for the modern reader is *The Parliament of Bees With their proper Characters* (1641) by John Daye, dedicated to his friend Charles Butler, who had addressed to 'the Muses' friends' his bee-keepers' treatise, *The Feminine Monarchie* (1609), combining refined humour, observation and learning with a tendency to humanize his creatures.[2] As in Drayton's poem, one member of the commonwealth acts as the king's representative, and as a social reformer seeks redress from him. Animal 'characters' had already appeared in *Partheneia Sacra* (Rouen, 1633), an emblem-book attributed to Henry Hawkins, and in *A Strange Metamorphosis of Man* (1634), attributed to Richard Braithwait,[3] but Daye was the first to devise a series of characters in verse, which manage to keep a fair balance between human and bee terms.[4]

Another somewhat less familiar pattern for the tale of the creatures was the elegy. At its simplest, this kind of poem was

---

[1] Thomas Blage, *A Schole of wise Conceytes*, no. 97, is a fable similar in detail. See also William Goddard, *A Satyricall Dialogue* (1616), 'The Owles arraygnement', and Richard Niccols, *The Beggers Ape* (1627), which also ends in a trial.

[2] George Wither wrote two introductory poems, one in Latin and one in English; (sig. A2ʳ):

> What *Recreation* better can befit
> Our grave *Divines*; then (when the Holy Writ
> Is laid aside) in Gods great book of *Creatures*
> To read his *Wisdome*, and their usefull *Natures*.

[3] Reprint ed. D. C. Allen (Baltimore, 1949).

[4] The description of this series of verse-characters as a play, which seems to have been first made by Arthur Symons, *Nero and other Plays* (Mermaid Series, 1880), was perpetuated by S. R. Golding, 'The Parliament of Bees', *R.E.S.* iii (1927), 280–304, in spite of Daye's own statement, 'To the Impartial Reader' (Symons, p. 214): 'my characters (or, if you will, colloquies)'.

a lament for a lost pet, of the sort composed by Drummond, Cartwright, and Herrick,[1] in recollection of classical and continental poets.[2] It might, however, lament the obsequies of some dead person symbolically (James VI's poem, 'Phoenix' is of this kind), or it might be both fiction and compliment, like 'The Metamorphosis of the Wallnut-tree of Borestall', by William Basse, a poem with its riddle, its explanation of origins, its list of mourners,[3] its will, and its moral application.

IV

The special challenge of a limited form was frequently appreciated by the Renaissance poet as a particular test of his sense of craftsmanship and of his versatility in producing new things from old. So to dispose one's mind towards a lineage of poems on the flea or the grasshopper as a tournament of ingenuities, a game played well, is to give them the sort of attention appropriate to them. Some poems within a tradition may offer more, when conventional patterns have caught alight through fresh perception; but a great many have to be read as jokes or illustrations of a platitude.

When Donne composed 'The Flea' he was being both more shocking and more serious than other poets who played with the thought of the pleasing death of some sort of fly at the hands of a lady, and the wish for metamorphosis from man to insect.[4] Drummond of Hawthornden[5] had somewhat spoiled the balance of sentiment in his versions of Tasso on this theme by transporting into them the idea of the martial prowess of

[1] See, for example, Drummond, *Works* (ed. cit., i. 102, 116; ii. 212); Cartwright, *Plays and Poems* (ed. cit., p. 477); Herrick, *Hesperides*, nos. 498, 968 (ed. cit., pp. 185, 302). For fuller discussion of Renaissance practice, see A. Lytton Sells, *Animal Poetry in French and English Literature and the Greek Tradition* (University of North Carolina, 1955).

[2] For example, Catullus, *Elegies* ii and iii; Statius, *Silvae*, ii. iv; Claudian, 'Phoenix'. Caspar Dornavius, *Amphitheatrum*, has many examples.

[3] Cf. Lovelace, 'The Falcon'; *Merry Drollery* (1670), 'A Combate of Cockes'.

[4] See Marcel Françon, 'Un Motif de la poésie amoureuse au XVIᵉ Siècle', *P.M.L.A.* lvi (1941), 307-36; and cf. *Greek Anthology*, v. 151, 152, the pseudo-Ovidian 'Carmen de Pulice', which appears in Caspar Dornavius's *Amphitheatrum*, *La Puce de Catherine Desroches* (Lyons, 1579), and Ronsard, *Amours* (1553), xli.

[5] Drummond, ed. cit. i. 125, from Tasso, *Rime* (Venice, 1608), iv. 104.

the fly, which had been recognized from Lucian onwards.[1] 'And if he die, he, knight-like, dies in blood.' The reader's attention is shifted from the banal or distasteful circumstances of the poem to a consideration of the smartness of its conceits. But Donne unflinchingly if subtly makes his readers aware of the naked fact, and yet somehow raises its importance in a way which other poets did not try to manage.

No other seventeenth-century poet attempted to define the intricacies of his relationship with his lady in this sort of poem with such *finesse*. There were plenty of poetic lovers who compared their fate to the death of a fly or a butterfly in the candle-light, in a steady, undistinguished Petrarchan manner.[2] There were plenty of playful compliments to the lady or to the insect itself for its good taste in choosing her, combining reflections on its amorous impudence with consideration of its death at her hand, or, more commonly, in her eye,[3] frequently with recollections of Martial's popular poems on creatures entombed in amber.[4] Like many dead creatures of the *Greek Anthology*, the fly was given a conceit of all-inclusiveness to describe its death.

> Thus she receiv'd from Celia's eye
> Funeral, flame, tomb, obsequy.[5]

The dominant tone in these poems is one of teasing

---

[1] 'Luciani Muscae Encomium' in Dornavius, op. cit., p. 117.

[2] See Mario Praz, *Studies in Seventeenth Century Imagery* (1939), p. 103, and cf. Erasmus, *Similia*, 616E, Hadrianus Junius, *Emblemata*, xlix, Samuel Daniel, *The worthy tract of Paulus Jovius . . . called Imprese*, sig. Biiii^v (1585), Camerarius, *Centuriae*, III. xcvii. See also in England, George Wither, *A Collection of Emblemes* (1635), I. xl, Robert Farlie, *Lychnocausia* (1638), xxv, Thomas Watson, *Hecatompathia* (c. 1582), xlviii, Bartholomew Griffin, *Fidessa* (1596), xxvi, Francis Davison, *A Poetical Rhapsody* (1602), 'Hee compares himselfe to a Candle-flie'.

[3] See Politian, 'Culicis Encomium', in *Epistolae*, xii, reprinted by Dornavius, op. cit., p. 116; Guarini, *Rime* (1598), fol. 76, madrigal xxxvii; Thomas Carew, *Poems* (1640), 'A Fly that flew into my Mistress her Eye', in *Poems* (Oxford, 1949), ed. Rhodes Dunlap, p. 37; William Cartwright, 'The Gnat', in *Poems and Plays*, ed. cit., p. 478; Robert Heath, *Clarastella* (1650), 'On a Fleabite espied on her fair hand'; *Musarum Deliciae* (1656), 'The Lowse's Peregrination', and 'Upon the biting of fleas'; Robert Fletcher, *Ex otio Negotium* (1656), 'Upon a Flye that flew into a Lady's eye, and there lay buried in a tear', p. 185. For the danger of playing in the king's eye, see Thomas Scot, *Philomythie*, 'Curiale', and Richard Lovelace, 'A Fly caught in a Cob-web', in *The Poems of Richard Lovelace*, ed. C. H. Wilkinson (Clarendon Press, Oxford, 1930), p. 155.

[4] iv. 32; iv. 59; vi. 15.   [5] Carew, ed. cit., p. 37.

whimsicality which might easily run to exaggeration and the grotesque. Herrick preferred a more tender amusement, and a style in which conceit was not over-played, but weighed finely against detail.

> A golden Flie one shew'd to me,
> Clos'd in a Box of Yvorie:
> Where both seem'd proud; the Flie to have
> His buriall in an yvory grave:
> The yvorie took State to hold
> A Corps as bright as burnisht gold.
> One Fate had both; both equall Grace;
> The Buried, and the Burying-place.
> Not *Virgils Gnat*, to whom the Spring
> All Flowers sent to 'is burying.
> Not *Marshals Bee*, which in a Bead
> Of *Amber* quick was buried
> Nor that fine Worme that do's interre
> Her selfe i' th' *silken Sepulchre*,
> Nor my rare *Phil*, that lately was
> With Lillies Tomb'd up in a Glasse;
> More honour had, then this same *Flie*;
> Dead, and clos'd up in *Yvorie*.[1]

The poem's relation to tradition is not entirely self-defined. Herrick might have known the poem in Dornavius's collection, 'Joannis Jacomoti, De Culice Globulo Succino sive Electro incluso',[2] which also appeared in Gruter's *Delitiae C Poetarum Gallorum* (Frankfurt, 1609).[3] He might also have read the essay, 'De Gemma Formicana' in the *Amphitheatrum*,[4] which

---

[1] *Hesperides*, no. 498 (ed. cit., p. 185).
[2] Op. cit., 117.   [3] ii. 370.
[4] P. 80. See *Musaeum Tradescantianum*, p. 36, 'Divers sorts of Ambers with Flyes, Spiders, naturall', in Sir John Tradescant's collection of rarities. Cf. also Sylvester's Du Bartas, ed. cit., p. 134, praise of a mechanical fly, and Robert Heath, 'On a Fleabite' (*Clarastella*, p. 24):

> And though for drawing so much guiltles bloud
>   Thou wel deserv'st to die,
> With a gold chain about thy neck, I wu'd
>   Have thee kept daintilie
> As *Scaliger's* was in a box; and shown
> As *Stella*'s gentle Fairie up and down.

Tradescant, op. cit., p. 39, lists 'Flea chains of silver and gold with 300 links a piece and yet but an inch long'.

described fossils and jewels containing insects, including beetles encased in gold. His poem is a fitting compliment to the easy relations between artifice and the creatures.

It is difficult to estimate how far each of these poems is related to particular models or predecessors, either English or continental, in the vernacular or in Latin. Yet the inspection of such anthologies as Gruter's and Dornavius's suggests that the English poets were aware of an European tradition, a kind of miniature Olympics in which they must each perform their own special feat. So Carew's poem, 'A Fly that flew into my Mistress her Eye', has affinities with poems of Politian and Guarini, and Cartwright's and Fletcher's English poems are variations on his. In another way, as a kind of anti-amatory rejoinder, Lovelace's poem, 'A Fly about a Glasse of Burnt Claret',[1] is also related to this group, for the claret plays the role of both eye and tear. It is 'The moist-hot glass and liquid fire', and the fly prefers the 'pleasing pain' of wine to love. Yet this poem has other more central associations. Lucian had mentioned the fly's certain death in oil, the *Greek Anthology* had an epigram about flies drowned in wine,[2] and the *Amphitheatrum* contained five epigrams concerning the fly which died in the king's golden dish, and was sculpted on a wine-bowl for remembrance.[3] Lovelace's conclusion, emphasizing the determination of the insect to run into danger again after being rescued, may also be paralleled in Latin.[4]

> I see! 'tis such a pleasing pain
> Thou wouldst be scorch'd and drown'd again.

[1] Ed. cit., p. 157.

[2] Cf. G. De La Perrière, *Le Théatre de bons engins* (Paris, 1561), iv, an emblem of flies drowned in milk. See also *Greek Anthology*, ix. 406, and Quevedo's poem, translated by Philip Ayres, *Lyric Poems* (1687), in *Minor Poets of the Caroline Period*, ed. G. Saintsbury (Clarendon Press, Oxford, 1906, 2 vols.), ii. 298. Frances Quarles, *Divine Fancies* (1632), p. 110, is an anti-potatory poem.

[3] P. 119. Cf. Drayton, *Muses Elizium*, 'The Eight Nimphall', describing 'A Cup in fashion of a Fly':

> At this Cups delicious brinke,
> A Fly approching but to drinke,
> Like Amber or some precious Gumme
> It transparent doth become.

[4] See Dornavius, op. cit., p. 117.

The poem, like others on the creatures by Lovelace, does not avoid the impression that in trying to over-reach himself and the tradition within which he stands, he falls into a strain of exaggeration in which fancy is not sufficiently disciplined by fine sentiment. In such poems, where invention is limited within small compass, the temptation to bombast is always strong; yet success is the more telling when it comes.

Andrew Marvell's poem, 'The Mower to the Glo-worms',[1] and Thomas Stanley's 'Stay fairest *Chariessa*',[2] seem also to have been written from some knowledge of an inheritance of literary associations. The glow-worm had a section to itself in the *Amphitheatrum*, which included an enigma by Scaliger[3] and an epigram by Antonius Thylesius Bonsentinus,[4] in which it is compared to a burning star, a fiery lamp, a piece of shining steel, and Proserpine leaving the underworld. Mantuan in one of his eclogues had written of the glow-worm flying with sparkling wings on spring evenings.[5] In France, Belleau had composed a brief poem, 'Le Ver Luisant', and in 'Le Con-templateur' St. Amant described it as a living star guiding his way home, a moving jewel, a fire which burned without being consumed.

The glow-worm inherited a double significance from classical writings. In Pliny, it was the shepherd's star, foretelling the harvest.[6] A cluster were like sparks of fire; they were a better zodiac, more fit to be studied than the heavens, and yet with the value of an earthly signature of the heavens.

Nature contented not her selfe to assemble a troup of starres together in a knot ... but she would needs give the Husbandman other starres beneath upon the earth, as signes to shew him the true seasons and times when and how to go to worke: as if she cried out and spake unto him after this manner: Why shouldest thou looke up to the heavens, thou that art to till the ground? Why keepest

---

[1] *Poems*, ed. H. M. Margoliouth, i. 44.

[2] In Stanley's 1647 and 1651 volumes it was placed first, but later omitted.

[3] P. 172; also in Reusner, *Aenigmatographia* (1599), p. 50.

[4] P. 172; also in Reusner, op. cit., p. 134, and in Moufet, *Theatrum Insectorum* (1634), p. 111.

[5] Quoted Dornavius, op. cit., p. 170.

[6] *Historia Naturalis* (Loeb Classical Library), XI. xxxiv. 98.

thou a seeking among the stars for thy countrey worke? Take thy rest and repose thy wearied lims good man, for the nights be now shorter than they were: to bed therefore, for thou hast but a while to sleep: Behold I scatter and spread here and there among thy very weeds and grasse growing upon the ground other especiall shining stars, and those I represent unto thine eies in the evening, and when thou doest unyoke and give order thy daies work: and that thou shouldest not either plead ignorance, or neglect the same, I provoke thee to regard and looke thereat, as a strange wonder.[1]

On the other hand, the insect was comparable to the traitor to the state, a false fire: this is how Cicero represented it.[2] Both these associations were known to writers of the Renaissance period, who used one or the other according to their purposes.

For the English poets, these insects were 'earth's poor stars . . . as thick as heav'ns',[3] they were 'those mites / Of Candi'd dew in Moony nights';[4] or they might be described as 'A moving diamond, a breathing stone'.[5] Some poets gave the creature moral associations which emphasized its brightness against the night. John Lyly showed a marked attachment to this kind of comparison. 'Dost thou not know that a perfect friende should be lyke the Glazeworme, which shineth most bright in the darke?'[6]

> O Stesias, what a heavenly love hast thou!
> A love as chaste as is Apolloes tree:
> As modest as a vestall Virgins eye,
> And yet as bright as Glowe wormes in the night.
> With which the morning deckes her lovers hair.[7]

Other qualities of the insect marked it out, however, as the deceiver. Like the powerful of this world, it shone by night

---

[1] Historia Naturalis, trans. by Philemon Holland as The Historie of the World, 2nd ed. (1634), XVIII. xxvii.

[2] Pro Publio Sestio, quoted in Dornavius, op. cit., p. 173.

[3] George Chapman, Eugenia (1614), 'Inductio'.

[4] Hesperides, no. 444, 'Oberon's Palace' (ed. cit., p. 165), to which Mildmay Fane's poem, 'The Fallacy of the outward Man', in Otia Sacra (1648), p. 48, is a moral retort. See Dornavius, op. cit., p. 171, on dew as the insect's origin.

[5] Edmund Waller, Poems (1645), 'Of and to the Queene'.

[6] Euphues (1579–80) in Works, ed. R. W. Bond, i. 234. Cf. Anthony Copley, A Fig for Fortune (1596), p. 22.

[7] The Woman in the Moone (1597), IV. i. 37–41; cf. Campaspe (1584), 'Epilogue'.

but its 'uneffectuall fire'[1] was extinguished by the sun; or it appeared to have heat which it did not possess, like false love.

> A man, near frozen with December's ire,
> Hath, from a heap of glowworms, as much ease
> As I can ever have by dreams as these.[2]

It is to Stanley's credit that he interwove several traditional associations without a major blunder, so that his poem is at once an essay in compression and in orderly procedure, each stanza ending with a witty point.

> Stay fairest Chariessa, stay and mark
> This animated Gem, whose fainter spark
> Of fading light, its birth had from the dark.

> A Star thought by the erring Passenger,
> Which falling from its native Orb dropt here,
> And makes the Earth (its Centre) now its Sphere.

> Should many of these sparks together be,
> He that the unknown light far off should see
> Would think it a terrestrial Galaxie.

> Take't up, fair Saint; see how it mocks thy fright!
> The paler flame doth not yield heat, though light,
> Which thus deceives thy Reason, through thy sight.

> But see how quickly it (ta'ne up) doth fade,
> To shine in darkness onely being made,
> By th' brightness of thy light turn'd to a shade;

> And burnt to ashes by thy flaming eyes
> On the chaste Altar of thy hand it dies,
> As to thy greater light a sacrifice.[3]

The comparison of insect to falling star is not original to Stanley, for it is recorded in the *Amphitheatrum*:[4] the thought is

---

[1] *Hamlet*, I. v. 90. Cf. Waller, op. cit., and *Amphitheatrum*, p. 173: 'Alius in Speculo animae peccatricis, petentes huius mundi cum Cicindella comparat, quae noctu obvolitans lucet, de die tota nigricat.'

[2] Browne, *Britannia's Pastorals*, III. i. 204–6. Cf. Bonsentinus's epigram, Phineas Fletcher, *Purple Island* (1633), viii. 5; *Pericles*, II. iii. 43; Habington, *Castara* (1634), 'To Castara, of true delight'; Samuel Sheppard, *Epigrams* (1651), p. 81.

[3] The 1647 version has 'This living star of earth' in the second line.

[4] Dornavius, op. cit., p. 171, 'dices coelestum igniculum in indignas terras delapsum'.

a natural extension of ideas found in Pliny. Even if Stanley had not himself handled a glow-worm, it was common book-knowledge that its light decreased as it was picked up.[1] This fact he combined cleverly with the sonneteers' identification of the beloved lady's eyes with the sun, before which the glow-worm conventionally paled. Aldrovandi had noted that it behaved towards the light in the same way as the butterfly.[2] Chariessa's votary thus joins the pyre with a host of other literary flies, its fate being appropriate both to believed fact and to tradition.

Like Stanley's poem, Marvell's has a pointedness and variety without loquacity; but Stanley's leaves an impression as cold as the insect on the hand, unlike the dolorous bewilderment of Marvell's final statement,

> For She my Mind hath so displac'd
> That I shall never find my home.

The poem begins with a juxtaposition of formality with familiarity. The insects he addresses as 'Ye living lamps', and there is a solemnity about the activity of the nightingale; yet there is affection in the phrase 'dear light'.

> Ye living Lamps, by whose dear light
> The Nightingale does sit so late,
> And studying all the Summer-night,
> Her matchless Songs does meditate.

There was an English proverb which ran 'You will make me believe that glowworms are lanterns',[3] and the Greek name 'Lampyrides' might easily suggest 'Lamps'. The idea that the insect provided light strong enough to read by was to be found in Gesner,[4] in Peter Martyr,[5] in Camerarius's collection of

---

[1] Dornavius, op. cit., p. 171.

[2] Ibid., p. 170. Bonsentinus mentioned how the insect flies obsequiously up to the faces of those watching it.

[3] See Tilley, *A Dictionary of Proverbs*, G. 143, and cf. *The Merry Wives of Windsor*, v. v. 82.

[4] Quoted by Camerarius, *Centuriae*, III. xciv, p. 93.

[5] Quoted by Moufet, *Theater of Insects* (1658), p. 977. 'Those that are without as well as they that have wings do send forth such a bright light, that by it you may read a great print. In this also they surpass Moon and Stars.' Martyr referred to Indians who worked by the light of 'this lanthorn of nature'.

emblems from the creatures, and in Moufet's *Theater of Insects*
—and it appeared satirically in Shadwell's play *The Virtuoso*
(1676).[1] 'I am now studying of Glow-worms, a fine Study; it
is a curious Animal. I think I shall preserve 'em light all the
year, and then I'll never use any other light in my Study but
Glow-worms and Concave-glasses.'

Marvell's glow-worm is the fairy-creature of Herrick ('Her
Eyes the Glow-worme lend thee'),[2] but its office is not a joyful
one like theirs. Instead, it gives light for the recollection of
unhappy love. The second stanza combines two traditional
ideas in a novel way.

> Ye Country Comets, that portend
> No War, nor Princes funeral,
> Shining unto no higher end
> Then to presage the Grasses fall.

Pliny had written much about the ominousness of the insect;
and Stanley's comparison of it with a comet has already been
noticed. The French poet, Belleau, came closest to Marvell's
thought, in his naming of the insect as the countryman's
prophet,

> Qui au laboureur prophètise
> Qu'il faut pour faucher aguise
> Sa faulx, et face les moissons.[3]

Marvell is more pointed than Belleau, not so diffuse. The
stanza is a variation on a theme beloved by him: the lives of
town and country run parallel, but as high to low ('Shining
unto no higher end'). The smallness of the insect and the short-
ness of grass are emblems of the humility associated with
country retirement, and even the portentousness of these
'Country Comets' is harmless.

Yet Marvell's insects are not uncivilized: their flame is
'officious', their lights are 'courteous'.[4] But the poet stands

---

[1] *Complete Works*, ed. Montague Summers (1927), iii. 164.
[2] *Hesperides*, no. 620, 'The Night-piece, to *Julia*' (ed. cit., p. 217).
[3] See *Œuvres*, ed. Pierre Gouverneur (Paris, 1876), i. 87.
[4] See *Arcadia*, ed. cit., p. 132:

> Saving the glowe worme, which would curteous be
> Of that small light oft watching shepheards see.

outside the general kindliness of nature and its civility, because he
has preferred to these meteors of good intent the 'foolish fires',
the deceptive meteors of love.[1]

> Ye Glo-worms, whose officious Flame
> To wandring Mowers shows the way,
> That in the Night have lost their aim,
> And after foolish Fires do stray;
>
> Your courteous Lights in vain you wast,
> Since *Juliana* here is come,
> For She my Mind hath so displac'd
> That I shall never find my home.

The poem is at once a continuation of tradition, and an alteration of it. Herrick's insect had guided his lady, Stanley's had
been subject to her, but Juliana is placed in opposition to the
glow-worm, and inferior to it in generosity, though superior
in her power over human beings. The fairy-world is not
adequate to cope with the larger world of 'War' and 'Princes
funeral' that lies above it, though it has its own orderliness;
and the poet's allegiance is divided. The worm has his affection,
and the lady his passion.

For the Greek poets, the grasshopper was the sweet singer,
the image of the poet himself, improvident, and yet sometimes
a symbol of deity,[2] and it was, of course, the carelessness of the
insect that Aesop harped upon.[3] It was Anacreon, however,
who was the important progenitor of English poems about the
grasshopper.[4] Though his poems were rendered into French
by Rémy Belleau in 1555, it took a hundred years for the same
to happen in England. Then three grasshopper-poems appeared
on one another's heels, Stanley's close rendering (1651),
Cowley's embroidery on Anacreon (1656), and Lovelace's

---

[1] 'The fire-drake' was conventionally feared by the wandering shepherd. See Ben
Jonson, 'The fiery beams upon you' (from *The Gipsies Metamorphosed*, 1640), Herrick's
model in 'The Night-piece, to *Julia*'.

[2] *Greek Anthology*, ix. 92. Thomas Moufet told his readers (*Theatrum Insectorum*,
1634, pp. 133–4) to consult the Greek and Latin epigrammatists on the insect. See also
Pierius Valerianus, *Hieroglyphica* (Lyons, 1610), XXVI. xli–xlvi.

[3] See Arnoldus Freitagius, *Mythologia Ethica* (Antwerp, 1579), p. 29. Geoffrey
Whitney, *A Choice of Emblemes* (Leyden, 1586), pp. 159, 175.

[4] *Carmina Anacreontea*, xliii.

PLATE V

Joachim Camerarius, *Symbolorum et Emblematum Centuriae* [1st edition],
III, xciv, Nuremberg, 1590

PLATE VI

Jacob Cats, *Proteus*, xlvii, The Hague, 1628

Make me to hear joy and gladness; that the bones
which Thou hast broken may rejoice. *Psalm li, 8*

poem, 'The Grassehopper', in *Lucasta* (1649), with a more complicated genealogy.

Stanley's rendering is not without verbal and metrical resemblances to Belleau's French version,[1] as well as many differences. Delight is subdued in the effort towards a correct rendering.

> Grasshopper thrice-happy! who
> Sipping the cool morning dew,
> Queen-like chirpest all the day
> Seated on some verdant spray;
> Thine is all whate'er earth brings,
> Or the hours with laden wings;
> Thee, the ploughman calls his joy,
> 'Cause thou nothing dost destroy:
> Thou by all art honour'd; all
> Thee the spring's sweet prophet call;
> By the Muses thou admir'd,
> By Apollo art inspir'd,
> Ageless, ever-singing, good,
> Without passion, flesh or blood;
> Oh how near thy happy state
> Comes the gods to imitate![2]

Cowley, on the other hand, turns Anacreon's straight statements into conceits. The language, only slightly metaphorical, of Stanley's fifth line, is brought nearer to mythological statement in

> *Nature* waits upon thee still,
> And thy verdant Cup does fill,
> 'Tis fill'd where ever thou dost tread,
> *Nature* selfe's *thy Ganimed.*[3]

Anacreon's delicate and perfect creature beyond humanity becomes at once an inhabitant of the Jacobean fairy-world, with its minute replicas of human utensils, and the symbol of

[1] Cf. 'prophet' with Belleau's 'Douce prophète de l'Esté', 'passion' and 'Franche de toute passion', mention of Apollo and the Muses and 'La Muse t'aime, et t'aime aussi Apollon'.

[2] *Anacreon: with Thomas Stanley's translation*, ed. A. H. Bullen (1893), p. 111.

[3] *Works* (1668), *Miscellanies*, p. 37, 'The Grashopper'.

a social ideal of the seventeenth century. It is taken from among
the lilies of the field to the epicurean's doorstep. The hint for
that perhaps is to be found in two epigrams from the *Anthology*, ix. 92, by Antipater of Thessalonica ('A little dew is
enough to make the cicada tipsy') and vii. 196, by Meleager.
They were both put into Latin during the sixteenth century;
and the number of renderings seems to reflect their popularity.[1]
In both, the insect is presented as 'drunken with dew-drops',
'Resonans cicada, roridis guttis ebria'. It was imitated by
Casimir Sarbiewski among his odes:[2]

> O quae populeâ summa sedens comâ,
> Caeli roriferis ebria lacrymis,
> Et te voce, *Cicada*,
> Et mutum recreas nemus.
> Post longas hiemes, dum nimiùm brevis
> Aestas se lenibus praecipitat rotis,
> Festinos, age, lento
> Soles excipe iurgio
> Ut se quaeque dies attulit optima,
> Sic se quaeque rapit: nulla fuit satis
> Umquam longa voluptas:
> Longus saepiùs est dolor.

This without doubt lies behind the first stanza of Lovelace's
poem 'The Grassehopper. To my Noble Friend, Mr. Charles
Cotton. Ode'.

> Oh thou that swing'st upon the waving haire
> Of some well-filled Oaten Beard,
> Drunke ev'ry night with a Delicious teare
> Dropt thee from Heav'n, where now th'art reard.[3]

[1] Hutton, *The Greek Anthology in France*, refers to two versions of vii. 196, and
The Greek Anthology in Italy (1935), records two. Dornavius, op. cit., p. 196, records
another. Of ix. 92, Hutton records one Latin version in Italy, three in France, and one
in vernacular French.

[2] Matthias-Casimir Sarbiewski, *Lyricorum libri IV* (Antwerp, 1632), iv. xxiii, 'Ad
Cicadam'.

[3] *Poems*, ed. C. H. Wilkinson (1930), p. 38. A translation of Sarbiewski, noted by
Wilkinson in *Poems of Lovelace* (1925), i. 30, appeared in *Miscellany Poems and Translations By Oxford Hands* (1685), p. 81, 'Blest Epicure of Race Divine', with text expanded
and altered to accord with the spirit of Cowley and Lovelace.

Cowley made some other transformations in the Anacreontic text. Aesop's warning is turned into Cowley's praise.

> Thou dost drink, and dance, and sing;
> Happier then the happiest *King*'

And the superiority of insect to man is carried in these lines:

> Man for thee does sow and plow;
> *Farmer He* and Land-Lord Thou!

The conclusion of the poem is bent towards the thought that the insect lives no longer than its happiness.

> To thee of all things upon earth,
> *Life* is no longer then thy *Mirth*.

This is not the thought of Anacreon, but rather of Pontanus in his Latin epigram.

> Cantando moritur; sentit nec taedia mortis.
> Quin cantu vitam ducit & exequias.
> O foelix ortu, interitu foelicior![1]

The life of Sarbiewski's insect is an emblem of pleasure. This, too, is the principal theme of Lovelace's poem, but his solution is contrary to the traditional one. Sarbiewski had added pathos to Aesop's stringent moral; and in Lovelace pity is prominent too. The grasshopper is both the comforter of man, and an intimation of human frailty. There is an irony about Lovelace's particular combination of traditional themes. Like the ant in Aesop, the poet is going to 'lay in 'gainst Winter, Raine', but only by prolonging the state appropriate to the grasshopper throughout the winter, after it is dead.

> Thou best of *Men* and *Friends*! we will create
> A Genuine Summer in each others breast.

The grasshopper is both a warning and a pattern, and it is only by paradox that the poet manages to keep the two halves of the poem together. The insect is 'Drunke ev'ry night'; so they will take refuge in 'an o'reflowing glasse'. It depended on heaven's showers; they will depend on 'show'rs of old Greeke'. The

[1] In Dornavius, op. cit., p. 170.

insect used to 'hop and flye', to sport in the sunshine,[1] they will 'play' in 'the light Casements'. The paradox is that men, by the same kind of activity as the insect, show themselves to be lords of nature and of themselves, whereas the grasshopper itself was a 'poore verdant foole'. They accomplish this by over-aweing its enemies: the 'sharpe frosty fingers' which destroy it are the 'frost-stretch'd Winges' which 'dissolve, and flye'. Ceres and Bacchus are in their glasses, when they have 'bid good night' to the insect, and the rain outside is allayed by their 'show'rs of old Greeke'.[2] The insect, like Cowley's, belongs to the fairy-world. The 'Carv'd Acron-bed' in which it lies belongs to the elves of *A Midsummer Night's Dream*.[3] Yet its fragility belongs rather to the moral emblem.

> Poore verdant foole! and now green Ice! thy Joys
> Large and as lasting, as thy Peirch of Grasse.

The grasshopper cannot perform miracles, and so becomes 'green Ice', whereas Lovelace and Cotton believe that they can 'poize / Their flouds, with an o'reflowing glasse'. There is even a slight hint of oxymoron in the last two words: stillness and motion are balanced against one another, life and deadness, in contrast to 'green Ice'. They are going to perpetuate the qualities of the insect without its hasty end.

If there is one of the creatures which for the sixteenth and seventeenth centuries is both absurd in essence and the carrier of divine mysteries, this is the ass. It had a load of opprobrious characteristics, both in proverbial speech and in fable. Pierius Valerianus gave a whole list of them in his *Hieroglyphica*:[4] it is ignorant of men and places, petulant and impudent, it is

---

[1] 'Sportst in the guilt-plats of his Beames' may be related to those poems in which the fly plays in the golden dish of the king.

[2] Hadrianus Junius, *Emblemata* (Leyden, 1596), xx (quoted P. Camerarius, *The Living Librarie*, translated John Molle (1625), III. vi, on poverty), makes the grasshopper an emblem of contentment and hope. See also J. Camerarius, *Centuriae*, III. xcvi, 'Expecto donec veniat', referring to Junius.

[3] II. i. 30–31:

> . . . that all their elves, for fear
> Creep into acorn-cups, and hide them there.

Cf. *Aeneid*, vi. 708, 'floribus insidunt variis'.

[4] Ed. cit., p. 115, 'Asinus'.

destitute of virtue, impatient, and so on. The man with the ass's ears is a favourite Renaissance symbol, deriving from Midas. (Topsell explored its significance in his natural history of the ass.)[1] And the ass which carries the image of Isis is a familiar emblem from Alciati[2] onwards, based on the Aesopic fable of Gabrias.[3]

> The seely asse bore on his backe
> Sainte Isis shrine they saye
> Eche man doth kneele and worshippe her,
> that metes her by the way.
> The asse gan to be proude, & saide
> this honor is to me.
> Not to thou Asse, but only that,
> thou bearest, worshippit be.
> God hath the calde to hye estate,
> thou beareste His shrine:
> Loke not alofte in thy conceyte,
> tis his, tis none of thyne.[4]

Thomas Scot's *Philomythie* included a fable called 'The Asse', in which he is at once critical of the animal and sympathetic towards it. It tells of a wild ass, once a courtier but metamorphosed as a result of his sins, which makes a covenant with a man. The ass keeps its part of the bargain and serves well, but the man breaks his. The whole tale is a warning against making covenants which are not observed, and has some relation to

---

[1] Op. cit., pp. 25–26.

[2] *Emblemata*, vii.

[3] The forty-three versified fables of Gabrias were frequently printed with the Planudean Aesop in Renaissance editions, with a Latin verse-translation. 'De Asino gestante simulacrum' was the sixth:

> Humeris Asinus gestabat simulacrum argenteum
> Quod unusquisque occurrens adorabat.
> Superbia vero elatus, nolens manere Asinus,
> Audivit: Non es to Deus, sed fers Deum.

This epigram was expanded to eight lines by Alciati.

[4] From the British Museum MS. of emblems, Sloane 3794, 'Two hundred poosees devysed by Thomas Palmer', fol. 41. Cf. Whitney, *A Choice of Emblemes*, p. 8. The ass represents the ignorant priest in William Alexander, *Poetical Works*, ed. Kastner and Charlton, ii. 223, and in Thomas Scot, *Philomythie*, 'The Asse'.

the *Golden Ass* of Apuleius (an English translation by William Aldington was published in 1566), and to a fable of Aesop.[1]

There is, however, another altogether tenderer view of the creature, related to its biblical heroism, which is represented by one of Crashaw's Latin *Sacra Epigrammata* (1634); 'Balaami Asinus':[2]

Matth. 21. 7.
In Asinum Christi vectorem.

Ille suum didicit quondam objurgare magistrum:
Et quid ni discas tu celebrare tuum?

Mirum non minùs est, te jam potuisse tacere,
Illum quàm fuerat tum potuisse loqui.

Encomia of the ass were not unpopular during the Renaissance period. Dornavius's *Amphitheatrum* included examples by Cornelius Agrippa, Jean Passerat, and Melanchthon; another by Heinsius appeared in 1623. In England, Agrippa's essay appeared at the end of James Sandford's translation, *Of the Vanitie and uncertaintie of Artes and Sciences* (1569), as 'A Digression in praise of the Asse', and Adriano Banchieri's *La Nobilta dell' Asino* was translated as *The Noblenesse of the Asse* (1595). Then Gabriel Harvey's *Pierces Supererogation* (1593) included 'A New Prayse of the Old Asse'. It was probably Cornelius Agrippa who popularized the knowledge that among the Hebrew Rabbis the the animal was reverenced as a symbol of wisdom, that Ammonius of Alexandria, a pupil of Origen, was called 'the ass', and that this was the name given to the early Christians by the Romans. Apuleius was moralized by him—the ass became the priest—and Balaam's animal was interpreted to represent the simple believing Christian. Of course the supreme ennoblement of the creature was its threefold appearance in the life of Christ, at His birth, the flight into Egypt, and the ride into Jerusalem. 'Atque ipse asinus etiam contactu corporis Christi consecratus est, crucisque signaculo insignatus.'

[1] 'Asinus et Hortulanus', commonly xlv. Cf. Thomas Blage, *A Schole of wise conceytes*, 'Of an Asse that served an unkinde Maister'; Freitagus, op. cit., p. 209, 'Permutata è meliore in peiorem conditio'.

[2] *Poetical Works*, ed. L. C. Martin (2nd ed. Clarendon Press, Oxford, 1957), p. 15.

By these thinges then whiche are already said, it is more manifest then ye sonne, that there is no beaste so able to receive divinitee as the Asse, into whome if yee shall not be tourned, yee shall not be able to carrie the divine misteries.[1]

Quarles had an undistinguished poem on the ass in his *Divine Fancies* (1632):

> The *Asse*, that for her slownesse, was forbid
> To be imployed in Gods service, did
> Performe good service now, in being slow:
> The *Asse* received stripes, but would not goe:
> She baulkd the way, and *Balam* could not guid her:
> The *Asse* had farre more wisedome then the *Rider*:
> The *Message* being bad, the *Asse* was loth
> To be the *Bearer*: 'Twas a happy sloth;
> 'Twas well for *Balam*: Had his *Asse* but tryde
> Another step, *Balam* had surely dy'd:
> Poore *Asse*! And was thy faithfull service payd
> With oft-repeated strokes? Hadst thou obayd,
> Thy Lord had bought thy travell, with his blood:
> *Such is Mans payment, often bad for Good:*
> The *Asse* begins to question with his *Master*,
> Argues the case, pleads why he went no faster:
> Nay, shewes him *Myst'ries*, far beyond his reach;
> *Sure, God wants Prophets, when dull* Asses *preach:*
> The *Asse* perceives the *Angel* and fals downe;
> When *Balam* sees him not; or sees, unknowne:
> Nor is't a wonder: for Gods *Spirit* did passe
> From blindfold *Balam*, into *Balams Asse*.[2]

Quarles seems to have remembered Alciati, and also the tale of the creature's ill-treatment; but it is Henry Vaughan who gives the fullest expression to this cluster of associations, in a poem unpretentious but with its own quiet order. The poet, as God's ass,[3] has been set in 'this busie street, / Of flesh and

---

[1] Sandford, op. cit., p. 185. [2] Op. cit., pp. 47–48.
[3] See the Spanish poem quoted and translated by James Howell, *The Parly of Beasts* (1660), p. 25:

> O happy *Asse* who God do'st bear,
> Such as Thou art, O wold I were.
> 'Tis said the man did pray so hard
> That prayer and person both were heard.

blood, where two ways meet', and given a law 'Which neither
tyres nor doth corrode, / But is a *Pillow*, not a *Load*'.

> Teach both mine eyes and feet to move
> Within those bounds set by thy love;
> Grant I may soft and lowly be,
> And minde those things I cannot see;
> Tye me to faith, though above reason,
> Who question power, they speak treason:
> Let me thy Ass be onely wise,
> To carry, not search mysteries;
> Who carries thee, is by thee led,
> Who argues, follows his own head.[1]

The poet himself is identified with the animal bearing Christ,
because it represents the condition of all faithful souls. The
mysteries of Alciati have become the awe which surrounds
Christ himself: so the emblem is drained of its bitterness. His
service will be for one Master only, and not for men and their
evil ways.

> Above all, make me love the poor,
> Those burthens to the rich man's door,
> Let me admire those, and be kinde,
> To low estates, and a low minde.

The idea of the covenant between man and animal is given its
just fulfilment in the entry into Jerusalem, in unelaborate lines,
matching the quality of Vaughan's piety. He may formerly
have run wild, but now, as Christ's 'poor foale' (the insect was
customarily known as 'poor fool'), he finds that the thistles of
this world would prick his lips, and longs for 'those Pastures
of life, where the Lamb goes'.[2] Agrippa had mentioned that
musicians made flutes from asses' bones, and this piece of lore
was repeated by Banchieri and others.[3] This odd detail became
the significant conclusion to Vaughan's poem.

---

[1] *Works*, ed. L. C. Martin, p. 518.
[2] In the Old Testament, wild asses represented erring Israel. The ass eating thistles
means the man of the world in Camerarius, *Centuriae*, II. lxxv (imitating Bochius).
[3] See Dornavius, op. cit., p. 494.

O let him by his *Lord* be led,
To living springs, and there be fed
Where light, joy, health, and perfect peace
Shut out all pain, and each disease;
Where death and frailty are forgotten,
And bones rejoyce, which once were broken!

In one ludicrous creature are discovered many important emblematic significances. Little has become much.

WERT thou thy life at libertie to choofe,
    And as thy birth, fo hadft thy beeing free,
The Citie thou fhouldft bid adieu, my Mufe,
And from her ftreetes, as her infection flee:
Where *CHAOS* and *CONFVSION* wee fee,
    Afwell of language, as of differing heartes,
    A bodie fevered in a thoufand parts.

➤ A wood neere Athens, wherein the Phylofophers vfed to ftudie.

Thy folitarie * Academe fhould be
Some fhadie groue, vpon the *THAMES* faire fide,
Such as we may neere princely *RICHMOND* fee,
Or where a long doth filuer *SEVERNE* flide,
Or *AVON* courtes, faire *FLORA* in her pride:
    There fhouldft thou fit at long defired reft,
    And thinke thy felfe, aboue a Monarch bleft,

3 · ORDER IN CONFUSION

Upon Appleton House, to my Lord Fairfax

I

WITHIN this sober Frame expect
Work of no Forrain *Architect*;
That unto Caves the Quarries drew,
And Forrests did to Pastures hew;
Who of his great Design in pain
Did for a Model vault his Brain,
Whose Columnes should so high be rais'd
To arch the Brows that on them gaz'd.[1]

II

Why should of all things Man unrul'd
Such unproportion'd dwellings build?
The Beasts are by their Denns exprest:
And Birds contrive an equal Nest;
The low roof'd Tortoises do dwell
In cases fit of Tortoise-shell:[2]
No Creature loves an empty space;
Their Bodies measure out their Place.

10

[1] Samuel Purchas, *Microcosmus* (1619), pp. 72–73: 'The most prominent parts of the *Forehead* (like the *Pent-houses, or goodly Arches, over the Windowes*) are the *Browes*.' Henry Hawkins, *Partheneia Sacra* (1633), 'The House', p. 166: 'A *House* being a meer artificial, and no natural thing, hath its first subsistence in the Idea of Man's brayne; according to whose model, good or il, the *house* so built, proves good or il.'

[2] The tortoise represents the self-contained man in George Wither, *A Collection of Emblemes* (1635), II. xxiv and IV. xiv.

PLATE VII

222

The beſt, and faireſt Houſe *to mee,*
Is that, where beſt I love to bee.

64

ILLVSTR. XIV.   Book.4

Hey are not *Houſes* builded large and high,
Seel'd all with *Gold,* and pav'd with *Porphyrie,*
Hung round with *Arras,* glaz'd with *Chriſtall-glaſſe,*
And cover'd o're with plates of ſhining *Braſſe,*
Which are the beſt; but, rather, thoſe where wee
In *ſaſetie, health,* and beſt *content,* may bee ;
And, where wee finde, though in a meane Eſtate,
That portion, which maintaines a quiet *Fate.*
  Here, in a homely *Cottage,* thatcht with reed,
The *Peaſant* ſeemes as pleaſedly to feed,
As hee, that in his *Hall* or *Parlour* dines,
Which Fret-worke Roofes, or coſtly Cedar Lines :
And, with the very ſame affections too,
Both to, and from it, hee doth come and goe.
The *Tortois,* doubtleſſe, doth no houſe-roome lack,
Although his *Houſe* will cover but his back;
And, of his *Tub,* the *Cynicke* ſeem'd as glad,
As *Alexander* was of all hee had.
When I am ſetled in a place I love,
A ſhrubby *hedge-row,* ſeemes a goodly *Grove.*
My liking maketh *Palaces* of *Sheds,*
And, of plaine *Couches,* carved Ivory *Beds :*
Yea, ev'ry *path,* and pathleſſe *walke,* which lies
Contemn'd, as rude, or wilde, in others eyes,
To mee is pleaſant ; not alone in ſhow,
But, truly ſuch : For, liking makes them ſo.
As pleas'd in theirs, the *Snailes,* and *Cocles* dwell,
As doth a *Scallop* in his pearly ſhell :
  For, that commends the *Houſe,* which makes it fir,
  To ſerve their turnes, who ſhould have uſe of it.

The

George Wither, *A Collection of Emblemes,* London, 1635

PLATE VIII

Theodore Beza, *Icones*, Geneva, 1580. From the copy in The National Library of Scotland

III

But He, superfluously spread,
Demands more room alive then dead.
And in his hollow Palace goes
Where Winds as he themselves may lose.   20
What need of all this Marble Crust
T'impark the wanton Mote of Dust,
That thinks by Breadth the World t'unite
Though the first Builders fail'd in Height?

IV

But all things are composed here
Like Nature, orderly and near:
In which we the Dimensions find
Of that more sober Age and Mind,
When larger sized Men did stoop
To enter at a narrow loop;   30
As practising, in doors so strait,
To strain themselves through *Heavens Gate*.[1]

V

And surely when the after Age
Shall hither come in *Pilgrimage*,
These sacred Places to adore,
By *Vere* and *Fairfax* trod before,
Men will dispute how their Extent
Within such dwarfish Confines went:
And some will smile at this, as well
As *Romulus* his Bee-like Cell.   40

VI

Humility alone designs
Those short but admirable Lines,

---

[1] *Cymbeline*, III. iii. 1-9.

By which, ungirt and unconstrain'd,
Things greater are in less contain'd.
Let others vainly strive t'immure
The *Circle* in the *Quadrature*![1]
These *holy Mathematicks* can
In ev'ry Figure equal Man.

VII

Yet thus the laden House does sweat,
And scarce indures the *Master* great: 50
But where he comes the swelling Hall
Stirs, and the *Square* grows *Spherical*;
More by his *Magnitude* distrest,
Then he is by its straitness prest:
And too officiously it slights
That in it self which him delights.

VIII

So Honour better Lowness bears,
Then That unwonted Greatness wears.
Height with a certain Grace does bend,
But low Things clownishly ascend.   60
And yet what needs there here Excuse,
Where ev'ry Thing does answer Use?
Where neatness nothing can condemn,
Nor Pride invent what to contemn?

IX

A Stately *Frontispice of Poor*
Adorns without the open Door:
Nor less the Rooms within commends
Daily new *Furniture of Friends.*

---

[1] Hebel tells Phalec how to prove 'the *Circles* Squareness', Sylvester, *Divine Weekes*,
p. 290. Cf. Purchas, *Microcosmus*, p. 540: 'And is not hee a very *Point*, and *Line*, and
Superficiall Man, that dwels in *Geometry*, and loseth himselfe *in quadraturo circuli*?'
Theodore Beza, *Icones* (Geneva, 1580), sig. Kk iv^v, has an emblem on square and circle.

The House was built upon the Place
Only as for *a Mark of Grace*;   70
And for an *Inn* to entertain
Its *Lord* a while, but not remain.

X

Him *Bishops-Hill*, or *Denton* may,
Or *Bilbrough*, better hold then they:
But Nature here hath been so free
As if she said leave this to me.
Art would more neatly have defac'd
What she had laid so sweetly wast;
In fragrant Gardens, shaddy Woods,
Deep Meadows, and transparent Floods.   80

XI

While with slow Eyes we these survey,
And on each pleasant footstep stay,
We opportunly may relate
The Progress of this Houses Fate.
A *Nunnery* first gave it birth.
For *Virgin Buildings* oft brought forth.
And all that Neighbour-Ruine shows
The Quarries whence this dwelling rose.

XII

Near to this gloomy Cloysters Gates
There dwelt the blooming Virgin *Thwates*;   90
Fair beyond Measure, and an Heir
Which might Deformity make fair.
And oft She spent the Summer Suns
Discoursing with the *Suttle Nunns*.
Whence in these Words one to her weav'd,
(As 'twere by Chance) Thoughts long conceiv'd.

XIII

'Within this holy leisure we
'Live innocently as you see.
'These Walls restrain the World without,
'But hedge our Liberty about.   100
'These Bars inclose that wider Den
'Of those wild creatures, called Men.
'The Cloyster outward shuts its Gates,
'And, from us, locks on them the Grates.

XIV

'Here we, in shining Armour white,
'Like *Virgin Amazons* do fight.
'And our chast *Lamps* we hourly trim,
'Lest the great *Bridegroom* find them dim.
'Our *Orient* Breaths perfumed are
'With insense of incessant Pray'r.   110
'And Holy-water of our Tears
'Most strangly our Complexion clears.

XV

'Not Tears of Grief; but such as those
'With which calm Pleasure overflows;
'Or Pity, when we look on you
'That live without this happy Vow.
'How should we grieve that must be seen
'Each one a *Spouse*, and each a *Queen*;
'And can in *Heaven* hence behold
'Our brighter Robes and Crowns of Gold?   120

XVI

'When we have prayed all our Beads,
'Some One the holy *Legend* reads;
'While all the rest with Needles paint
'The Face and Graces of the *Saint*.

'But what the Linnen can't receive
'They in their Lives do interweave.
'This Work the *Saints* best represents;
'That serves for *Altar's Ornaments.*

XVII

'But much it to our work would add
'If here your hand, your Face we had: 130
'By it we would *our Lady* touch;
'Yet thus She you resembles much.
'Some of your Features, as we sow'd,
'Through ev'ry *Shrine* should be bestow'd.
'And in one Beauty we would take
'Enough a thousand *Saints* to make.

XVIII

'And (for I dare not quench the Fire
'That me does for your good inspire)
''Twere Sacriledge a Man t'admit
'To holy things, for *Heaven* fit.   140
'I see the *Angels* in a Crown
'On you the Lillies show'ring down:
'And round about you Glory breaks,
'That something more then humane speaks.

XIX

'All Beauty, when at such a height,
'Is so already consecrate.
'*Fairfax* I know; and long ere this
'Have mark'd the Youth, and what he is.
'But can he such a *Rival* seem
'For whom you *Heav'n* should disesteem?   150
'Ah, no! and 'twould more Honour prove
'He your *Devoto* were, then *Love.*

XX

'Here live beloved, and obey'd:
'Each one your Sister, each your Maid.
'And, if our Rule seem strictly pend,
'The Rule it self to you shall bend.
'Our *Abbess* too, now far in Age,
'Doth your succession near presage.
'How soft the yoke on us would lye,
'Might such fair Hands as yours it tye!　　　　160

XXI

'Your voice, the sweetest of the Quire,
'Shall draw *Heav'n* nearer, raise us higher.
'And your Example, if our Head,
'Will soon us to perfection lead.
'Those Virtues to us all so dear,
'Will straight grow Sanctity when here:
'And that, once sprung, increase so fast
'Till Miracles it work at last.

XXII

'Nor is our *Order* yet so nice,
'Delight to banish as a Vice.　　　　170
'Here Pleasure Piety doth meet;
'One perfecting the other Sweet.
'So through the mortal fruit we boyl
'The Sugars uncorrupting Oyl:
'And that which perisht while we pull,
'Is thus preserved clear and full.

XXIII

'For such indeed are all our Arts;
'Still handling Natures finest Parts.
'Flow'rs dress the Altars; for the Clothes,
'The Sea-born Amber we compose;　　　　180

'Balms for the griv'd we draw; and Pasts
'We mold, as Baits for curious tasts.
'What need is here of Man? unless
'These as sweet Sins we should confess.

XXIV

'Each Night among us to your side
'Appoint a fresh and Virgin Bride;
'Whom if *our Lord* at midnight find,
'Yet Neither should be left behind.
'Where you may lye as chast in Bed,
'As Pearls together billeted.   190
'All Night embracing Arm in Arm,
'Like Chrystal pure with Cotton warm.[1]

XXV

'But what is this to all the store
'Of Joys you see, and may make more!
'Try but a while, if you be wise:
'The Tryal neither Costs, nor Tyes.'
Now *Fairfax* seek her promis'd faith:
Religion that dispensed hath;
Which She hence forward does begin;
The *Nuns* smooth Tongue has suckt her in.   200

XXVI

Oft, though he knew it was in vain,
Yet would he valiantly complain.
'Is this that *Sanctity* so great,
'An Art by which you finly'r cheat?
'Hypocrite Witches, hence *avant*,
'Who though in prison yet inchant!
'Death only can such Theeves make fast,
'As rob though in the Dungeon cast.

[1] *Arcadia*, ed. cit., p. 221:
> For there with strange compact dooth lie
> Warme snow, moyst pearle, softe ivorie.

XXVII

'Were there but, when this House was made,
'One Stone that a just Hand had laid,   210
'It must have fall'n upon her Head
'Who first Thee from thy Faith misled.
'And yet, how well soever ment,
'With them 'twould soon grow fraudulent:
'For like themselves they alter all,
'And vice infects the very Wall.

XXVIII

'But sure those Buildings last not long,
'Founded by Folly, kept by Wrong.
'I know what Fruit their Gardens yield,
'When they it think by Night conceal'd.   220
'Fly from their Vices.   'Tis thy state,
'Not Thee, that they would consecrate.
'Fly from their Ruine.   How I fear
'Though guiltless lest thou perish there.'

XXIX

What should he do?   He would respect
Religion, but not Right neglect:
For first Religion taught him Right,
And dazled not but clear'd his sight.
Sometimes resolv'd his Sword he draws,
But reverenceth then the Laws: 230
For Justice still that Courage led;
First from a Judge, then Souldier bred.

XXX

Small Honour would be in the Storm.
The *Court* him grants the lawful Form;
Which licens'd either Peace or Force,
To hinder the unjust Divorce.

Yet still the *Nuns* his Right debar'd,
Standing upon their holy Guard.
Ill-counsell'd Women, do you know
Whom you resist, or what you do?   240

XXXI

Is not this he whose Offspring fierce
Shall fight through all the *Universe*;
And with successive Valour try
France, *Poland*, either *Germany*;
Till one, as long since prophecy'd,
His Horse through conquer'd *Britain* ride?
Yet, against Fate, his Spouse they kept;
And the great Race would intercept.

XXXII

Some to the Breach against their Foes
Their *Wooden Saints* in vain oppose.   250
Another bolder stands at push
With their old *Holy-Water Brush*.
While the disjointed *Abbess* threads
The gingling Chain-shot of her *Beads*.
But their lowd'st Cannon were their Lungs;
And sharpest Weapons were their Tongues.

XXXIII

But, waving these aside like Flyes,
Young *Fairfax* through the Walls does rise.
Then th' unfrequented Vault appear'd,
And superstitions vainly fear'd.   260
The *Relicks false* were set to view;
Only the Jewels there were true.
But truly bright and holy *Thwaites*
That weeping at the *Altar* waites.

XXXIIII

But the glad Youth away her bears,
And to the *Nuns* bequeaths her Tears:
Who guiltily their Prize bemoan,
Like Gipsies that a Child hath stoln.
Thenceforth (as when th'Inchantment ends
The Castle vanishes or rends)   270
The wasting Cloister with the rest
Was in one instant dispossest.

XXXV

At the demolishing, this Seat
To *Fairfax* fell as by Escheat.
And what both *Nuns* and *Founders* will'd
'Tis likely better thus fulfill'd.
For if the *Virgin* prov'd not theirs,
The *Cloyster* yet remained hers.
Though many a *Nun* there made her Vow,
'Twas no *Religious House* till now.   280

XXXVI

From that blest Bed the *Heroe* came,
Whom *France* and *Poland* yet does fame:
Who, when retired here to Peace,
His warlike Studies could not cease;
But laid these Gardens out in sport[1]
In the just Figure of a Fort;
And with five Bastions it did fence,
As aiming one for ev'ry Sense.

---

[1] Country life is associated with innocent mirth by Sarbiewski, *Lyricorum libri IV*,
ed. cit., p. 215, 'Laus otii religiosi':

> innocentibus jocis,
> Multoque tinctus, sed verecundo sale,
> Innoxium trahit diem.

XXXVII

When in the *East* the Morning Ray
Hangs out the Colours of the Day,[1]   290
The Bee through these known Allies hums,
Beating the *Dian* with its *Drumms*.[2]
Then Flow'rs their drowsie Eylids raise,
Their Silken Ensigns each displayes,
And dries its Pan yet dank with Dew,
And fills its Flask with Odours new.[3]

XXXVIII

These, as their *Governour* goes by,
In fragrant Vollyes they let fly;[4]
And to salute their *Governess*
Again as great a charge they press: 300
None for the *Virgin Nymph*; for She
Seems with the Flow'rs a Flow'r to be.
And think so still! though not compare
With Breath so sweet, or Cheek so faire.

---

[1] Marlowe, *Tamburlaine, Part II*, III. i. 47:

> That on mount Sinai, with their ensigns spread,
> Look like the parti-coloured clouds of heaven
> That show fair weather to the neighbour morn.

[2] Cleveland, 'Fuscara: or, The Bee Errant' (1651):

> Tuning his draughts with drowsy hums,
> As Danes carouse by kettle-drums.

[3] Flowers are often militarized in the verse of the period, particularly by Giles and Phineas Fletcher. See *Purple Island* (1633), vi. 68; *Elisa* (1633), ii. 34. *Partheneia Sacra* has this conceit in abundance.

[4] Drayton, *The Muses Elizium* (1630), 'The sixt Nimphall':

> The motlied Meadowes then, new vernisht with the Sunne
> Shute up their spicy sweets upon the winds that runne.

'The eight Nimphall':

> Shute your sweets into the ayre,
> Charge your morning to be fayre.

XXXIX

Well shot ye Firemen! Oh how sweet,
And round your equal Fires do meet;[1]
Whose shrill report no Ear can tell,
But Ecchoes to the Eye and smell.[2]
See how the Flow'rs, as at *Parade*,
Under their *Colours* stand displaid: 310
Each *Regiment* in order grows,
That of the Tulip Pinke and Rose.

XL

But when the vigilant *Patroul*
Of Stars walks round about the *Pole*,
Their Leaves, that to the stalks are curl'd,
Seem to their Staves the *Ensigns* furl'd.
Then in some Flow'rs beloved Hut
Each Bee as Sentinel is shut;
And sleeps so too: but, if once stir'd,
She runs you through, or askes *the Word*.   320

XLI

Oh Thou, that dear and happy Isle[3]
The Garden of the World ere while,
Thou *Paradise* of four Seas,
Which *Heaven* planted us to please,

---

[1] Flowers were frequently compared to fires by the Fletchers, and by Benlowes, their imitator.

[2] Henry Vaughan, *Silex Scintillans*, 'The Queer':
> A wing with eyes, and eyes that taste.

The mingling of the senses is common in Joshua Poole, *English Parnassus* (1657). Habington liked the device, and Samuel Butler satirizes it in 'The Elephant in the Moon'.

[3] *Richard II*, III. iv. 43–44, 75–76.
> When our sea-walled garden, the whole land,
> Is full of weeds, her fairest flowers chok'd up.

> What Eve, what serpent, hath suggested thee
> To make a second fall of cursed man?

But, to exclude the World, did guard
With watry if not flaming Sword;
What luckless Apple did we tast,
To make us Mortal, and The Wast?

XLII

Unhappy! shall we never more
That sweet *Militia* restore,   330
When Gardens only had their Towrs,
And all the Garrisons were Flowrs,
When Roses only Arms might bear,
And Men did rosie Garlands wear?
Tulips, in several Colours barr'd,
Were then the *Switzers* of our *Guard*.

XLIII

The *Gardiner* had the *Souldiers* place,
And his more gentle Forts did trace.
The Nursery of all things green
Was then the only *Magazeen*.[1]   340
The *Winter Quarters* were the Stoves,
Where he the tender Plants removes.
But War all this doth overgrow:
We Ord'nance Plant and Powder sow.

XLIV

And yet their walks one on the Sod
Who, had it pleased him and *God*,
Might once have made our Gardens spring
Fresh as his own and flourishing.

---

[1] 'Magazine' meant for the seventeenth century a store-house of riches. Ben Jonson and Donne used it of people, to mean an epitome of delights. In *Partheneia Sacra* the garden is a 'Magazin . . . of perfumes': here it is particularly a military store-house. 'Nursery' means both a place for young plants and a place of origin.

But he preferr'd to the *Cinque Ports*[1]
These five imaginary Forts: 350
And, in those half-dry Trenches, spann'd
Pow'r which the Ocean might command.

XLV

For he did, with his utmost Skill,
Ambition weed, but *Conscience* till.
Conscience, that Heaven-nursed Plant,
Which most our Earthly Gardens want.[2]
A prickling leaf it bears, and such
As that which shrinks at ev'ry touch;
But Flowrs eternal, and divine,
That in the Crowns of Saints do shine.   360

XLVI

The sight does from these *Bastions* ply,
Th' invisible *Artilery*;
And at proud *Cawood Castle* seems
To point the *Battery* of its Beams.
As if it quarrell'd in the Seat
Th' Ambition of its *Prelate* great.
But ore the Meads below it plays,
Or innocently seems to gaze.

XLVII

And now to the Abbyss I pass
Of that unfathomable Grass,   370
Where Men like Grashoppers appear,
But Grashoppers are Gyants there:

---

[1] *Loves Martyr*, Jonson's 'Epos': 'th'Eye and Eare (the Ports unto the Mind)';
Scot, *Philomythie* (1616), sig. B3ᵛ: 'Make not your will warden of your Cinque Ports';
Purchas, *Microcosmus*, p. 83: the senses are 'the *Cinque Ports* of this Region'; Quarles,
A Feast for Wormes (1630), 'The Eye (the chiefest Cinque-port of the Heart)'.
[2] Cf. Southwell, 'Love's Gardyne Griefe'; Joseph Beaumont, 'The Gardin'.

They, in there squeking Laugh, contemn
Us as we walk more low then them:
And, from the Precipices tall
Of the green spir's, to us do call.[1]

XLVIII

To see Men through this Meadow Dive,
We wonder how they rise alive.
As, under Water, none does know
Whether he fall through it or go.   380
But, as the Marriners that sound,
And show upon their Lead the Ground,
They bring up Flow'rs so to be seen,
And prove they've at the Bottom been.

XLIX

No Scene that turns with Engines strange
Does oftner then these Meadows change.
For when the Sun the Grass hath vext,
The tawny Mowers enter next;
Who seem like *Israalites* to be,
Walking on foot through a green Sea.   390
To them the Grassy Deeps divide,
And crowd a Lane to either Side.

L

With whistling Sithe, and Elbow strong,
These Massacre the Grass along:
While one, unknowing, carves the *Rail*,
Whose yet unfeather'd Quils her fail.
The Edge all bloody from its Breast
He draws, and does his stroke detest;
Fearing the Flesh untimely mow'd
To him a Fate as black forebode.   400

[1] Nathaniel Wanley, *Scintillulae Sacrae* (1634), ed. L. C. Martin (1928), p. 41:
Clodds turn'd to starres; each tender spire of grasse
A monarchy that should the Roman passe.

LI

But bloody *Thestylis*, that waites
To bring the mowing Camp their Cates,
Greedy as Kites has trust it up,
And forthwith means on it to sup:
When on another quick She lights,
And cryes, he call'd us *Israelites*;
But now, to make his saying true,
Rails rain for Quails, for Manna Dew.[1]

LII

Unhappy Birds! what does it boot
To build below the Grasses Root;   410
When Lowness is unsafe as Hight,
And Chance o'retakes what scapeth spight?
And now your Orphan Parents Call
Sounds your untimely Funeral.[2]
Death-Trumpets creak in such a Note,
And 'tis the *Sourdine* in their Throat.

LIII

Or sooner hatch or higher build:
The Mower now commands the Field;
In whose new Traverse seemeth wrought
A Camp of Battail newly fought: 420
Where, as the Meads with Hay, the Plain
Lyes quilted ore with Bodies slain:
The Women that with forks it fling,
Do represent the Pillaging.

---

[1] Sylvester, ed. cit., p. 112: 'Some *Rail*, or *Quail*, or *Partridge* would she bring';
p. 114: '*Mel* and *Manna*'.

[2] *Georgics*, iv. 511–15: lament of parent bird; Giles Fletcher, *Christs Triumph over Death*, lxvii. Henry Peacham, *Minerva Britanna*, lxxxv: partridges caught by their mother's error represent a kingdom ruined by a bad king.

LIV

And now the careless Victors play,
Dancing the Triumphs of the Hay;
Where every Mowers wholesome Heat
Smells like an *Alexanders sweat*.
Their Females fragrant as the Mead
Which they in *Fairy Circles* tread: 430
When at their Dances End they kiss,
Their new-made Hay not sweeter is.

LV

When after this 'tis pil'd in Cocks,
Like a calm Sea it shews the Rocks:
We wondring in the River near
How Boats among them safely steer.
Or, like the *Desert Memphis Sand*,
Short *Pyramids* of Hay do stand.
And such the *Roman Camps* do rise
In Hills for Soldiers Obsequies.   440

LVI

This *Scene* again withdrawing brings
A new and empty Face of things;
A levell'd space, as smooth and plain,
As Clothes for *Lilly* strecht to stain.
The World when first created sure
Was such a Table rase and pure.
Or rather such is the *Toril*
Ere the Bulls enter at Madril.

LVII

For to this naked equal Flat,
Which *Levellers* take Pattern at,[1]   450
The Villagers in common chase
Their Cattle, which it closer rase;

[1] Davenant's universal herd in *Gondibert*, vi. lx, 'play, whilst yet their Tyrant is unmade'.

And what below the Sith increast
Is pincht yet nearer by the Beast.
Such, in the painted World, appear'd
Davenant with th' Universal Heard.

LVIII

They seem within the polisht Grass
A Landskip drawen in Looking-Glass.
And shrunk in the huge Pasture show
As Spots, so shap'd, on Faces do.   460
Such Fleas, ere they approach the Eye,
In Multiplying Glasses lye.
They feed so wide, so slowly move,
As *Constellations* do above.

LIX

Then, to conclude these pleasant Acts,
Denton sets ope its *Cataracts*;
And makes the Meadow truly be
(What it but seem'd before) a Sea.
For, jealous of its *Lords* long stay,
It try's t'invite him thus away.   470
The River in it self is drown'd,[1]
And Isl's th' astonish'd Cattle round.

LX

Let others tell the *Paradox*,
How Eels now bellow in the Ox;
How Horses at their Tails do kick,
Turn'd as they hang to Leeches quick;
How Boats can over Bridges sail;
And Fishes do the Stables scale.
How *Salmons* trespassing are found;
And Pikes are taken in the Pound.   480

---

[1] *Metamorphoses*, x. 291–312; Drayton, *Noah's Floud* (1630).

LXI

But I, retiring from the Flood,
Take Sanctuary in the Wood;
And, while it lasts, my self imbark
In this yet green, yet growing Ark;[1]
Where the first Carpenter might best
Fit Timber for his Keel have Prest.
And where all Creatures might have shares,
Although in Armies, not in Paires.

LXII

The double Wood of ancient Stocks
Link'd in so thick, an Union locks,   490
It like two *Pedigrees* appears,
On one hand *Fairfax*, th' other *Veres*:
Of whom though many fell in War,
Yet more to Heaven shooting are:[2]
And, as they Natures Cradle deckt,
Will in green Age her Hearse expect.

LXIII

When first the Eye this Forrest sees
It seems indeed as *Wood* not *Trees*:
As if their Neighbourhood so old
To one great Trunk them all did mold.   500
There the huge Bulk takes place, as ment
To thrust up a *Fifth Element*;
And stretches still so closely wedg'd
As if the Night within were hedg'd.

---

[1] Benlowes, *Sphinx Theologia* (1636), p. 16:
> Arca Creaturas vasti tenet unica Mundi;
> Quod medio quaeras gurgite, littus habet.
Cowley, *Miscellanies* (1668), 'Of Wit':
> As in the *Ark*, joyn'd without force or strife,
> All *Creatures* dwelt; all *Creatures* that had *Life*.
Cowley, 'The Garden', st. vi, the ark represents 'Nature's Liberalitie'.

[2] 'Shoot' is used of trees by Spenser (*Faerie Queene*, II. v. 31–32). The tree shooting to heaven, with the motto 'Prospiciente Deo' appears in Camerarius, *Centuriae*, I. iii.

LXIV

Dark all without it knits; within
It opens passable and thin;
And in as loose an order grows,
As the *Corinthean Porticoes*.
The arching Boughs unite between
The Columnes of the Temple green;   510
And underneath the winged Quires
Echo about their tuned Fires.

LXV

The *Nightingale* does here make choice
To sing the Tryals of her Voice.
Low Shrubs she sits in, and adorns
With Musick high the squatted Thorns.
But highest Oakes stoop down to hear,[1]
And listning Elders prick the Ear.
The Thorn, lest it should hurt her, draws
Within the Skin its shrunken claws.[2]   520

LXVI

But I have for my Musick found
A Sadder, yet more pleasing Sound:
The *Stock-doves*, whose fair necks are grac'd
With Nuptial Rings their Ensigns chast;[3]

[1] Cowley, 'Of Solitude':
> 'Hail, old *Patrician* Trees, so great and good!
> Hail ye *Plebeian* under wood!'

[2] Habington, 'To Castara Ventring to walke too farre in the neighbouring Wood': 'The courteous thicket'. Jane Barker, *Poetical Recreations* (1688), 'Upon a Flock of Gold-Finches Seen in the Morning':
> The *Thorns* themselves shrunk in to make them room,
> And sheath'd their prickles in their barky Womb.

[3] Camerarius, op. cit. III. lx: doves on a marriage-pyre (cf. 'The Phoenix and the Turtle': 'a mutual flame'); III. lxiii: faithful union of turtle-doves, with Horace, *Odes*, I. xiii as an epigraph: 'Felices ter & amplius / Quos irrupta tenet copula.' Marvell's doves wear their 'Nuptial Rings' round their necks.

PLATE IX

Iuſtitia omnibus partibus ab-
ſoluta.

Deum time), & mandata eius obſerua: hoc eſt enim omnis homo. Eccleſ. 12, 13.

FINIS.

Arnold Freitag, *Mythologia Ethica*, Antwerp, 1579

Yet always, for some Cause unknown,
Sad pair unto the Elms they moan.
O why should such a Couple mourn,
That in so equal Flames do burn!

LXVII

Then as I carless on the Bed
Of gelid *Straw-berryes* do tread,   530
And through the Hazles thick espy
The hatching *Thrastles* shining Eye,
The *Heron* from the Ashes top,
The eldest of its young lets drop,
As if it Stork-like did pretend
That *Tribute* to *its Lord* to send.

LXVIII

But most the *Hewel's* wonders are,
Who here has the *Holt-felsters* care.
He walks still upright from the Root,
Meas'ring the Timber with his Foot;   540
And all the way, to keep it clean,
Doth from the Bark the Wood-moths glean.
He, with his Beak, examines well
Which fit to stand and which to fell.

LXIX

The good he numbers up, and hacks;
As if he mark'd them with the Ax.
But where he, tinkling with his Beak,
Does find the hollow Oak to speak,

That for his building he designs,
And through the tainted Side he mines.   550
Who could have thought the *tallest Oak*[1]
Should fall by such a *feeble Strok'*!

LXX

Nor would it, had the Tree not fed
A *Traitor-worm*, within it bred.
(As first our *Flesh* corrupt within
Tempts impotent and bashful *Sin*.
And yet that *Worm* triumphs not long,
But serves to feed the *Hewels young*.
While the Oake seems to fall content,
Viewing the Treason's Punishment.   560

LXXI

Thus I, *easie Philosopher*,
Among the *Birds* and *Trees* confer:
And little now to make me, wants
Or of the *Fowles*, or of the *Plants*.
Give me but Wings as they, and I
Streight floting on the Air shall fly:
Or turn me but, and you shall see
I was but an inverted Tree.[2]

LXXII

Already I begin to call
In their most learned Original: 570
And where I Language want, my Signs
The Bird upon the Bough divines;

---

[1] Howell, 'Before the Second Part of Dodona's Grove':
            When a fresh breeze did blow, and reinspire
            Their leafs with language like an Orphean lyre,
            To tell the gazing World what a dire stroak,
            Or fatall clap of thunder crush'd the *Oke*.
Dodona's oak in Howell's work represents Charles I.
[2] Purchas, *Microcosmus*, p. 340: man is like an inverted tree.

PLATE X

L'HOMME EST VN ARBRE RETOVRNE. 35

Tout arbre qui ne fait pas bon fruit, fera coupé,&
jetté au feu. Matth.3. c.

K 2

Geerhardt de Jode, Μικρόκοσμος, Anvers, 1589

PLATE XI

EMBLEMA

TANGOR, NON FRANGOR AB VNDIS.

Jacob Cats, *Silenus Alcibiadis*, Amsterdam, 1630

And more attentive there doth sit
Then if She were with Lime-twigs knit.
No Leaf does tremble in the Wind
Which I returning cannot find.

LXXIII

Out of these scatter'd *Sibyls* Leaves
Strange *Prophecies* my Phancy weaves:[1]
And in one History consumes,
Like *Mexique Paintings*, all the *Plumes*.[2]   580
What *Rome*, *Greece*, *Palestine*, ere said
I in this light *Mosaick* read.
Thrice happy he who, not mistook,
Hath read in *Natures mystick Book*.

LXXIV

And see how Chance's better Wit
Could with a Mask my studies hit!
The Oak-Leaves me embroyder all,
Between which Caterpillars crawl:
And Ivy, with familiar trails,
Me licks, and clasps, and curles, and hales.   590
Under this *antick Cope* I move
Like some great *Prelate of the Grove*,

LXXV

Then, languishing with ease, I toss
On Pallets swoln of Velvet Moss;
While the Wind, cooling through the Boughs,
Flatters with Air my panting Brows.

---

[1] 'Propheticke trees' were not uncommon in contemporary poems; a wood in *Arcadia* had 'a Mosaicall floore'.

[2] Tradescant, *Musaeum Tradescantianum*, p. 41: 'Divers sorts of pictures wrought in feathers.'

Thanks for my Rest ye *Mossy Banks*,
And unto you *cool Zephyr's* Thanks,
Who, as my Hair, my Thoughts too shed,
And winnow from the Chaff my Head.   600

LXXVI

How safe, methinks, and strong, behind
These Trees have I incamp'd my Mind;
Where Beauty, aiming at the Heart,
Bends in some Tree its useless Dart;
And where the World no certain Shot
Can make, or me it toucheth not.
But I on it securely play,
And gaul its Horsemen all the Day.

LXXVII

Bind me ye *Woodbines* in your 'twines,
Curle me about ye gadding *Vines*,   610
And Oh so close your Circles lace,
That I may never leave this Place:
But, lest your Fetters prove too weak,
Ere I your Silken Bondage break,
Do you, O *Brambles*, chain me too,
And courteous *Briars* nail me through.

LXXVIII

Here in the Morning tye my Chain,
Where the two Woods have made a Lane;
While, like a *Guard* on either side,
The Trees before their *Lord* divide;   620
This, like a long and equal Thread,
Betwixt two *Labyrinths* does lead.
But, where the Floods did lately drown,
There at the Ev'ning stake me down.

LXXIX

For now the Waves are fal'n and dry'd,
And now the Meadows fresher dy'd;
Whose Grass, with moister colour dasht,
Seems as green Silks but newly washt.[1]
No *Serpent* new nor *Crocodile*
Remains behind our little *Nile*;   630
Unless it self you will mistake,
Among these Meads the only Snake.

LXXX

See in what wanton[2] harmless folds
It ev'ry where the Meadow holds;
And its yet muddy back doth lick,
Till as a *Chrystal Mirrour* slick;
Where all things gaze themselves, and doubt
If they be in it or without.
And for his shade which therein shines,
Narcissus like, the *Sun* too pines.[3]   640

LXXXI

Oh what a Pleasure 'tis to hedge
My Temples here with heavy sedge;
Abandoning my lazy Side,
Stretcht as a Bank unto the Tide;

---

[1] *The Tempest*, II. i. 65–68: 'That our garments being (as they were) drencht in the
Sea, hold notwithstanding their freshnesse and glosses, being rather new-dy'de then
stain'd with salte water.'

[2] 'Wanton' is used pejoratively by Spenser for the Bower of Bliss (*Faerie Queene*, II.
xii. 53: 'wanton wreathings intricate').

[3] Fairfax, 'The Solitude' from St. Amant (Bodleian MS., Fairfax 38, p. 552):

> Sometimes soe cleare & so serene
> Itt seemes ast were a looking glass
> And to our vewes preventing seemes
> As heaven beneath the water was
> The sun in it's soe clearly seene
> That contemplating this bright sight
> As't was a doubt whether itt had beene
> Himsellf or Image gave the Light
> Att first appearing to our eyes
> As if he had falne from the skyes.

Or to suspend my sliding Foot
On the Osiers undermined Root,
And in its Branches tough to hang,
While at my Lines the Fishes twang!

LXXXII

But now away my Hooks, my Quills,
And Angles, idle Utensils.   650
The *young Maria* walks to night:
Hide trifling Youth thy Pleasures slight.
'Twere shame that such judicious Eyes
Should with such Toyes a Man surprize;
She that already is the *Law*
Of all her *Sex*, her *Ages Aw*.

LXXXIII

See how loose Nature, in respect
To her, it self doth recollect;
And every thing so whisht and fine,
Starts forth with to its *Bonne Mine*.   660
The *Sun* himself, of *Her* aware,
Seems to descend with greater Care;
And lest *She* see him go to Bed;
In blushing Clouds conceales his Head.

LXXXIV

So when the Shadows laid asleep
From underneath these Banks do creep,
And on the River as it flows
With *Eben Shuts* begin to close;

PLATE XII

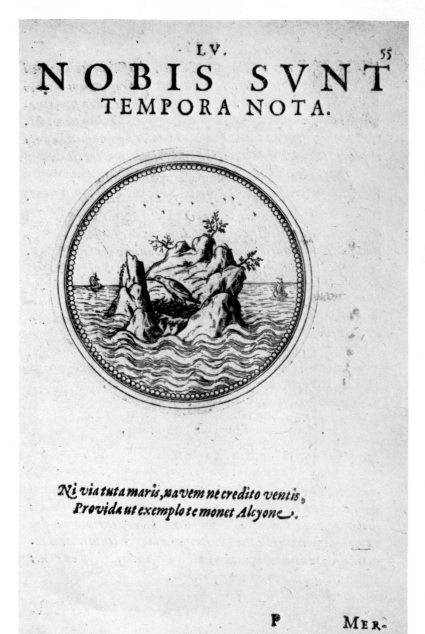

Joachim Camerarius, *Symbolorum et Emblematum Centuriae* [1st edition], III, lv, Nuremberg, 1590

The modest *Halcyon* comes in sight,
Flying betwixt the Day and Night;[1]   670
And such an horror calm and dumb,
Admiring Nature does benum.[2]

LXXXV

The viscous[3] Air, wheres'ere She fly,
Follows and sucks her Azure dy;
The gellying Stream compacts below,
If it might fix her shadow so;

---

[1] St. Basil, *Hexaemeron*, viii, and St. Ambrose, *Hexaemeron*, v. xiii, described the kingfisher's nesting-habits. Erasmus used the bird several times in his *Parabolarum, sive similium liber* (Strasbourg, 1516): 'Ut halcyones etiam media hyeme mare tranquillum praestant nonsibi solum sed aliis quoque: Ita sapiens turbatissimis rebus non solum ipse tuebitur animi tranquillitatem, sed alio concitatos componit ac sedabit.' The halcyon in Alciati, clxxviii, represents the king who preserves peace and prosperity:

> Laetus erit Cereri, Baccho quoque fertilis annus,
> Aequorei si rex alitis instar erit.

In Paulus Jovius it represents the nobles of Geneva ('Nous savons bien le temps'); in Camerarius, *Centuriae*, III. lv, it is the type of a wise man 'qui in mediis Rep. procellis sibi prospicere, et quietiora ac tranquilliora tempora expectare novit'. The emblem is appropriate to Fairfax himself in his retirement from warfare: his daughter's power over his country-retreat is like his over the nation.

[2] Central to Théophile de Viau's poem 'La Maison de Sylvie', translated in part by Thomas Stanley in his *Poems and Translations* (1651) as 'Sylvia's Park', is the theme of the lady's magical influence over the landscape, particularly in the evening.

> Whilst with one hand the Line she cast,
>   Commanding Silence with the other,
> Her signe the Day obeying, past
>   More slily by her dusky Brother.
> The doubtful Sun with equal awe,
> Fear'd to approach or to withdraw:
>   The intentive Stars suspend their glowing.
> No Rage the quiet Billows swell'd,
> *Favonius* his soft breath withheld,
>   The listning Grass refrain'd from growing.

[3] 'Viscous' and 'gellying' are both words belonging to the discussion of meteors. Cf. lxxxvi.

The stupid Fishes[1] hang, as plain
As *Flies* in *Chrystal* overt'ane;
And Men the silent *Scene* assist,
Charm'd with the *Saphir-winged Mist*,[2]   680

LXXXVI

Maria such, and so doth hush
The *World*, and through the *Ev'ning* rush.
No new-born *Comet* such a Train
Draws through the Skie, nor Star new-slain.
For streight those giddy Rockets fail,
Which from the putrid Earth exhale,
But by her *Flames*, in *Heaven* try'd,
Nature is wholly *vitrifi'd*.

LXXXVII

'Tis *She* that to these Gardens gave
That wondrous Beauty which they have;   690
She streightness on the Woods bestows;
To *Her* the Meadow sweetness owes;
Nothing could make the River be
So Chrystal-pure but only *She*;
She yet more Pure, Sweet, Streight, and Fair,
Then Gardens, Woods, Meads, Rivers are.

[1] *Stupid*, stupified. In Gruter, *Delitiae C. Poetarum Gallorum* (1609), iii. 137. 'In piscem glacie inclusum' the fish lives and dies in water, whereas the poet lives on earth, and dies in love's fire. For the enclosure of things in glass see Martial IV. xxii (lilies in crystal), VIII. lxviii (grapes in glass, limbs in silk, pebbles in water); Sylvester, *Divine Weekes*, Bersabe is 'Like to a Lillie sunk into a glasse'; Harington, *Orlando Furioso*, VII. xxvi.

[2] In Picinelli, *Mundus Symbolicus* (trans. A. Erath, Cologne, 1681), p. 267, the blue colour of the sapphire is described as so intense that it transfers itself to what is close to it: *Quae tangit, caerula reddit.* In Bartholomaeus Anglicus, *De proprietatibus rerum*, trans. by John Trevisa (1535) XVI. lxxxvii, the sapphire, whose colour is heavenly, reconciles opposites and preserves chastity.

LXXXVIII

Therefore what first *She* on them spent,
They gratefully again present.
The Meadow Carpets where to tread;
The Garden Flow'rs to Crown *Her* Head;   700
And for a Glass the limpid Brook,
Where *She* may all *her* Beautyes look;
But, since *She* would not have them seen,
The Wood about *her* draws a Skreen.

LXXXIX

For *She*, to higher Beauties rais'd,
Disdains to be for lesser prais'd.
She counts her Beauty to converse
In all the Languages as *hers*;
Nor yet in those *her self* imployes
But for the *Wisdome*, not the *Noyse*;   710
Nor yet that *Wisdome* would affect,
But as 'tis *Heavens Dialect*.

LXXXX

Blest Nymph! that couldst so soon prevent
Those *Trains* by Youth against thee meant;
Tears (watry Shot that pierce the Mind;)
And *Sighs* (Loves Cannon charg'd with Wind;)
True Praise (That breaks through all defence;)
And *feign'd complying Innocence*;
But knowing where this *Ambush* lay,
She scap'd the safe, but roughest Way.   720

LXXXXI

This 'tis to have been from the first
In a *Domestick Heaven* nurst,
Under the *Discipline* severe
Of *Fairfax*, and the starry *Vere*;

Where not one object can come nigh
But pure, and spotless as the Eye;
And *Goodness* doth it self intail
On *Females*, if there want a *Male*.

LXXXXII

Go now fond Sex that on your Face
Do all your useless Study place,   730
Nor once at Vice your Brows dare knit
Lest the smooth Forehead wrinkled sit:
Yet your own Face shall at you grin,
Thorough the Black-bag of your Skin;
When *knowledge* only could have fill'd
And *Virtue* all those *Furrows till'd*.

LXXXXIII

Hence *She* with Graces more divine
Supplies beyond her *Sex* the *Line*;
And, like a *sprig of Misleto*,
On the *Fairfacian Oak* does grow;   740
Whence, for some universal good,
The *Priest* shall cut the sacred Bud;
While her *glad Parents* most rejoice,
And make their *Destiny* their *Choice*.

LXXXXIV

Mean time ye Fields, Springs, Bushes, Flow'rs,
Where yet She leads her studious Hours,
(Till Fate her worthily translates,
And find a *Fairfax* for our *Thwaites*)
Employ the means you have by Her,
And in your kind your selves preferr;   750
That, as all *Virgins* She preceds,
So you all *Woods, Streams, Gardens, Meads*.

LXXXXV

For you *Thessalian Tempe's Seat*
Shall now be scorn'd as obsolete;
Aranjuez, as less, disdain'd;
The *Bel-Retiro* as constrain'd;
But name not the *Idalian Grove*,
For 'twas the Seat of wanton Love;
Much less the Dead's *Elysian Fields*,
Yet nor to them your Beauty yields.   760

LXXXXVI

'Tis not, what once it was, the *World*;
But a rude heap together hurl'd;
All negligently overthrown,
Gulfes, Deserts, Precipices, Stone.
Your lesser *World* contains the same.
But in more decent Order tame;
You Heaven's Center, Nature's Lap.
And Paradice's only Map.

LXXXXVII

But now the *Salmon-Fishers* moist
Their *Leathern Boats* begin to hoist;   770
And, like *Antipodes* in Shoes,
Have shod their *Heads* in their *Canoos.*
How *Tortoise like*, but not so slow,
These rational *Amphibii* go?
Let's in: for the dark *Hemisphere*
Does now like one of them appear.

A Vale of Teares

IN this landscape poem by the Jesuit Robert Southwell (1561–95) traditional contemplation contains auguries of the Augustan sublime. Yet in its appreciation of 'disordered order' the poem belongs firmly to its time.

The text of *Moeoniae* (1595) has been followed, except where the Stonyhurst type manuscripts, as described by James H. McDonald, *The Poem*

and Prose Writings of Robert Southwell, a Bibliographical Study (Roxburghe
Club, Oxford, 1937), or the 1634 version give better readings. In one case
a suggestion by W. B. Turnbull, *The Poetical Works of Robert Southwell*
(1856), has been followed.

A VALE there is enwrapt with dreadfull shades,
Which thicke of mourning pines shrouds from the sunne
Where hanging clifts yeld short and dumpish glades,
And snowy flouds with broken streames do runne,
Where eie-roume is from rocke to cloudie skie,
From thence to dales which stormy ruines shrowd,
Then to the crushed waters frothie frie,
Which tumbleth from the tops where snow is thow'd:
Where eares of other sound can have no choice,
But various blustring of the stubborne wind,
In trees, in caves, in straits with divers[1] noise,
Which now doth hisse, now howle, now roare by kinde
Where waters wrastle with encountering stones,
That break their streames, and turne them into foame,
The hollow clowds ful fraught with thundering groans
With hideous thumps discharge their pregnant wombe.
And in the horror of this fearfull quier,
Consists the musicke of this dolefull place:
All pleasant birds their tunes from thence retire,
Where none but heavy notes have any grace.
Resort there is of none but pilgrim wights,
That passe with trembling foote and panting hearte,
With terrour cast in cold and shuddring frights,
They judge the place[2] to terror framde by art:
Yet natures worke it is of arte untoucht,
So straite indeede, so vaste unto the eie,
With such disordred order strangely coucht,
And so with pleasing horror low and hie,
That who it viewes must needes remaine agast,
Much at the worke, more at the makers might,
And muse how Nature such a plot could cast,

---

[1] *divers* 1634, otherwise *diver.*
[2] *And all the place* 1595.

Where nothing seemed wrong, yet nothing right:
A place for mated mindes, an onely bower,
Where everie thing doth soothe a dumpish mood.
Earth lies forlorne, the cloudie skie doth lower,
The wind here weeps, here sighes, here cries aloude:
The strugling floud between the marble grones,
Then roaring beates upon the craggie sides,
A little off a midst the pibble stones,
With bubling streams & purling noise it glides.[1]
The pines thicke set, hie growne, and ever greene,
Still cloath the place with shade and mourning vaile.
Here gaping cliffes, there mosse growne plaine is seene,
Here hope doth spring, and there againe doth quaile.
Huge massie stones that hang by tickle stay,
Still threaten foule, and seeme to hang in feare,
Some withered trees ashamed of their decay,
Beset with greene, and forcde gray cotes to weare.
Here christall springes crept out of secret vaine,
Straite finde some envious hole that hides their grace,[2]
Here seared tufts[3] lament the want of rayne,[4]
There thunder wracke gives terror to the place.
All pangs and heavie passions here may find
A thousand motives suting[5] to their griefes,
To feede the sorowes of their troubled mind,
And chase away dame pleasures vaine releefes.
To plaining thoughts this vaile a rest may bee,
To which from worldly toyes they may retire,
Where sorrow springs from water, stone, and tree,
Where everie thing with mourners doth conspire.
Sett here my soule mayn streames of tears aflote,[6]
Here all thy sinfull toyles alone recount,
Of solemne tunes make thou the dolefulst note,

---

[1] & purling noyse Stonyhurst, a purling noise 1595.
[2] finde . . . grace Stonyhurst, findes . . . graine 1595.
[3] seared tufts Turnbull, for feared tufts.
[4] want of rayne Stonyhurst, wants of grace 1595.
[5] suting 1634 suitly.
[6] Sett . . . aflote Stonyhurst, Sit here my soule, mourne streames of teares afloate 1595.

That to thy ditties dolor may amount.
When *Eccho* doth repeate thy painfull cries,
Thinke that the verie stones thy sinnes bewray,
And now accuse thee with their sad replies,
As heaven and earth shall in the latter day:[1]
Let former faults be fuell of the fire,
For griefe in Limbecke of thy heart to still[2]
Thy pensive thoughts, and dumps of thy desire,
And vapour teares up to thy eies at will.
Let teares to tunes, and paines to plaints be prest,
And let this be the burthen to thy song,
Come deep remorse, possesse my sinful brest:
Delights adue, I harbored you too long.

I

As the valleys are more aboundant and bring forth more fruit then
the mountaines do, by reason that being more lowe, they receive
more commodiouslie all the dewe and fatnesse which falleth and
descendeth from the hie hils: even so it behooveth that we bee
lowe and humble in our own eies, if wee will, that God replenish us
with his graces, the which can find no place in us, if wee presume
any whit of our vertues.[3]

The emblematic significance of hill and valley and the contrast
between them were sixteenth-century commonplaces of the
sort which some seventeenth-century poets still found useful
and important when they came to write about landscape. Two
poems in particular receive some fresh light from the recognition of this: these are George Denham's *Cooper's Hill* and
Andrew Marvell's 'Upon the Hill and Grove at Bill-borrow'.
    Although Mantuan's eighth eclogue was probably the most
easily accessible poetic treatment of the theme of hill and valley
for Elizabethan readers,[4] he was only following the habit

---

[1] colon 1634, otherwise comma.
[2] 1634 omits period.
[3] Francis Meres, *Palladis Tamia* (1598), fol. 97ᵛ.
[4] See George Turbervile, *The eclogs turned into English verse* (1567, 1572); *The Bucolicks* (1656); *Mantuan English'd* (1680). See also Tilley, *A Dictionary of Proverbs*, H 467, 'There is no Hill without its valley'; V 7, 'The Vale best discovers the hill'.

PLATE XIII

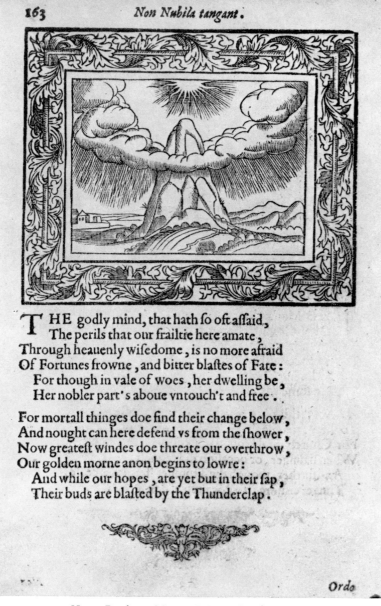

163   *Non Nubila tangant.*

T HE godly mind, that hath so oft assaid,
     The perils that our frailtie here amate,
Through heauenly wisedome, is no more afraid
Of Fortunes frowne, and bitter blastes of Fate:
     For though in vale of woes, her dwelling be,
     Her nobler part's aboue vntouch't and free.

For mortall thinges doe find their change below,
And nought can here defend vs from the shower,
Now greatest windes doe threate our overthrow,
Our golden morne anon begins to lowre:
     And while our hopes, are yet but in their sap,
     Their buds are blasted by the Thunderclap.

Ordo

Henry Peacham, *Minerva Britanna*, London, 1612

preserved in the prose of Bartholomaeus Anglicus[1] and in *The dialoges of creatures moralysed.*[2]

The mountain was both fact and symbol; and Spenser, not unexpectedly, allowed its emblematic qualities to have more prominence. 'Julye' of the *Shepheardes Kalendar* is his reply to Mantuan, in disapproval of Roman saint-worship, pomp, and prelacy. There is not much originality about his account of mountain-life, if his application is ingenious. His details are those of Bartholomaeus. The lowly plain preferred by Thomalin is the Church of the Reformation, the area of humility and faithful shepherding. Thomas Churchyard presents another side of the argument in 'A discourse of Mountaynes',[3] which is part of *Worthines of Wales* (1587). The valley represented the simple life for Spenser; but Churchyard combined personal knowledge and image-making in enumerating the virtues of the hardy life, in which storms are accompanied by content. He gives the other side of Bartholomaeus's picture, and moralizes in the manner of *The dialoges of creatures*: servants should be subject to their masters. Nor could the vales do without the protection of the hills, as the commons could not do without the king.

> You may compare, a King to Mountayne hye,
> Whose princely power, can byde both bront and shocke
> Of bitter blast, or Thunderbolt from Skye,
> His Fortresse stands, upon so firme a Rocke.
> A Prince helps all, and doth so strongly sit,
> That none can harme, by fraude, by force nor wit.
> The weake must leane, where strength doth most remayne,
> The Mountayne great, commaunds the little Playne.[4]

Churchyard's description of mountain-life is at once a realistic account of country stoicism, brought in to support the familiar

---

[1] *De proprietatibus rerum*, translated by John Trevisa (1535); Stephen Batman, *Batman uppon Bartholome* (1582), XIV. ii, xxviii, xxxvi, xlvii. See also St. Basil, *Hexaemeron*, IX. v.

[2] Dialogue vii, 'Of the Hyll and the Valey' (Antwerp, 1534, sig. D2).

[3] Sigs. M1ʳ-M3ʳ.

[4] Sig. M2ᵛ.

idea 'That sweet content, with Oten cakes can live', and an emblematic defence of kingship.

Preference for the valley was a common feature of pastoral poetry. It might refer to the choice of the base rather than the mean or the epic style,[1] or to the choice of a state of humility rather than proud aloofness,[2] or of rustic retirement rather than the competitive scramble of the town. The poets had discovered the paradox expressed by Robert Southwell in a moral poem, 'In lowly vales I mount / To Pleasure's highest pitch',[3] and by William Basse in a pastoral eclogue, that contentment is 'the grace / Of greatnes, Greatnes of inferiour place'.[4]

Michael Drayton found the debate between hill and valley convenient to give some kind of formal structure to *Poly-Olbion*. His own individual contribution to it is his praise of the middle state, represented by Malvern in the Seventh Song and by the hill called Mein in the Fourteenth, whose name no doubt appealed to him because of the opportunity for an emblematic pun: 'Of all the Hills I knowe, let *Mein* thy pat-terne bee.'[5] It combines the graces of field and forest, and as the seat of 'deere Clifford' 'many a time hath been the Muses quiet Port'.

Another idea which he puts forward is that hills and valleys are interdependent. This is the point of the debate in the Ninth Song between the mountain-nymphs of Merionethshire who praise their home and the water-nymphs of Lin-teged who reply that mountains did not exist before the flood. (This Selden denied in a note.) The conclusion is appeasement by Snowdon, and a friendly strife of compliment between vales and hills. 'They only now contend, which most should other grace.'[6] The Vale of Evesham in the Fourteenth Song reiterates the thought that hills cannot do without valleys, either for use

---

[1] See W. Browne, *The Shepheards Pipe* (1614), v. 67–86; *Britannia's Pastorals*, II. i. 886–96.

[2] See Camerarius, *Centuriae*, I. lxxiii; Henry Peacham, *Minerva Britanna*, lv.

[3] 'Content and Ritche' in *Complete Poems of Robert Southwell*, ed. A. Grosart, 1872, p. 72.

[4] Basse, ed. cit., 'Clio', eclogue iii.

[5] *Poly-Olbion*, xiv. 157.   [6] Ibid., ix. 374.

or for beauty's sake. Consideration will prove 'what lofty Hills to humble Valleys owe'.[1] This is not so far from the idea which was becoming commonplace around 1600, that pleasing effects are obtained through the juxtaposition of opposites. 'So all agreed, through sweete diversitie.'[2]

The very grasp of how to weave a sentence from one couplet to another distinguishes Denham from his predecessors. A sense of economy, of logicality, of development, makes his poem a superior one. Yet it is still more of an emblem of kingship than a description. Like Drayton, Denham took a middle place in the debate between mountain and valley, for his royal figures share the qualities of both. He chose several eminences to comment through them on the various aspects of kingship. St. Paul's is the city-mountain; and the poet has made sure by strong insinuation that his readers should grasp this:

> so vast, so high,
> That whether 'tis a part of Earth, or sky,
> Uncertain seems, and may be thought a proud
> Aspiring mountain, or descending cloud.
> Under his broad survey the City lies,
> And like a mist beneath a hill doth rise;
> Whose state and wealth the business and the crowd,
> Seems at this distance but a darker cloud.[3]

Churchyard and Drayton had connected the valley with commerce and the production of clouds, which were later borne by the hills. St. Paul's represents the monarch as lofty protector, standing amidst the city and state affairs, and yet undisturbed by the world beneath.[4] Windsor, on the other hand, represents the monarch in relation to love and honour. Images of feminity

---

[1] Ibid. xiv. 130.

[2] Faerie Queene, II. xii. 59. Cf. Arcadia (1590), ed. cit., p. 91. See also H. V. S. Ogden, 'The Principles of Variety and Contrast in Seventeenth Century Aesthetics, and Milton's Poetry', J.H.I. x (1949), 159–82.

[3] 15–18, 25–28 (1655 ed.) Cf. Poly-Olbion, vii. 89, 'For Mountaines be like Men of brave heroïque mind'; Britannia's Pastorals, I. iv. 355–6; John Weever, Faunus and Melliflora (1600), sig. B2ᵛ.

[4] See Peacham, Minerva Britanna, clxi.

and masculinity, of domesticity and military prowess are combined. The 'gentle height' of the hill at Windsor is itself emblematic of the king's character. If the recent discovery that the description of the hill has a close relation to Sarbiewski's ode to the Duke of Bracciano is an illuminating one,[1] there are nevertheless important differences between the two poems. For Denham's wit, though in the same vein, is considerably subtler. In both, a castle symbolic of military power stands on a slowly rising hill,[2] suggesting an interrelation of courtesy and strength. But the hill at Windsor seems to suggest two things—not only the king's own balanced character, but also his marriage—and the description of the hill is arranged to have this ambiguous reference. So when we read that here 'Mars with Venus dwells. Beauty with strength', we are aware that this might refer to king and queen or to the king alone. The hill at Windsor is also made to conform to the aristocratic ideal of the Carolines, for whom there is 'No honour truly high that scorns the low'. There is a hint of this in Denham's phrase, 'an easie and unforc't ascent'. The *New English Dictionary* cites this as the first example of the use of 'unforced' to mean 'requiring or involving no physical exertion'. Is it not possible that Denham's extension of meaning is due to a punning recollection of Queen Gertrude's words to Hamlet, attributing to him a 'gentle and unforced accord'?[3]

In the next part of the poem, a neighbouring hill arouses reflections on the destruction of buildings caused by Henry VIII, and on contemporary politics. The Thames is overlaid with human similes, comparing it to human life and kingship, each of which might be split off from the other as an emblematic

---

[1] M.–S. Røstvig, *The Happy Man. Studies in the Metamorphoses of a Classical Ideal, 1600–1700* (Oslo, 1954), p. 146. The ode, 'Ad Paulum Jordanum Ursinum Bracciani Ducem. Braeciani agri amoenitatem commendat, ad quam per ferias Septembres secesserat Roma' appeared in Casimir Sarbiewski, *Lyricorum Libri IV*. ed. cit., pp. 205–11, and in translation by George Hill, *The Odes of Casimire*, pp. 105–21.

[2] Cf. Claudian, *De raptu Proserpinae*, ii. 101–3, 'curvata tumore / parvo planities et mollibus edita clivis / creverat in collem'; Sarbiewski, 'Clemens supino clivus assurgit iugo, / Caelumque paulatim subit'; *Poly-Olbion*, xiv. 33–38, on the Lickey, whose 'height seem'd slowly but to rise', and whose 'swelling soyle' did not 'like other hills to suddaine sharpnesse mount'.

[3] *Hamlet*, I. ii. 123, and cf. *Coriolanus*, II. ii. 28 and *The Tempest*, II. i. 120.

epigram. Such is the 'morality too frequent' with which Dr. Johnson found fault, and which John Dennis praised.[1] Then without any fuss the poet slips into a passage recognizable as a defence of landscape which includes both mountains and plains.

> Such huge extreams when Nature doth unite,
> Wonder from thence results, from thence delight.[2]

Nature herself is witty, so that Denham is imitating her precedent in the uniting of extremes, in the making of oxymoron, of paradox, and of abstruse, emblem-like similes. As an account of poetic procedure, these lines have as much validity as his frequently quoted lines on the river's course. Nature in this poem is the genius both decorous and surprising.

> Wisely she knew, the harmony of things,
> As well as that of sounds, from discords springs.[3]

In 'Upon the Hill and Grove at Bill-borrow' Marvell was also at work refining traditional clumsiness through wit. His poem is the Commonwealth version of the theme of humble leader, with Lord Fairfax, his patron, as the subject of praise. The symbolic shapes of mountains and the circularity of the earth before the Flood both appear in *Poly-Olbion*; but in his first stanza Marvell made flat statement into paradox, comparing the hill to the world without hills.

> See how the arched Earth does here
> Rise in a perfect Hemisphere!
> The stiffest Compass could not strike
> A Line more circular and like;
>
> . . . . .
>
> It seems as for a Model laid,
> And that the World by it was made.[4]

---

[1] See Johnson, *Lives of the Poets*, 'Denham', and Dennis, *Works*, ed. cit., ii. 135–7.
[2] 211–12. [3] 203–4.
[4] *Poems and Letters*, ed. H. M. Margoliouth, i. 56. Cf. *Richard II*, III. ii. 153, 'That small model of the barren earth' (of a grave-mound), and *Poly-Olbion*, xxi. 89–92:

> For Nature in your shapes, notoriously did erre
> But skillfull was in me, cast pure Orbiculer.
> Nor can I be compar'd, so like to any thing,
> By him that would express my shape, as to a Ring.

His way of improving upon the traditional language about hills and extending old meanings is by punning on them.

> Nor softest Pensel draw a Brow
> So equal as this Hill does bow.

'Brow' and 'Model' express Marvell's continual preference for nature rather than the lady whose portraiture was a not uncommon subject for complimentary poems. Shapes and anatomy again coalesce in the second stanza: hills are both unshapely bodies and geographical features. The old identification of mountain and ruler is extended by being combined with pastoral diction and cosmology, possibly with a recollection of Richard Crookback:

> Here learn ye Mountains more unjust,
> Which to abrupter greatness thrust,
> That do with your hook-shoulder'd height
> The Earth deform and Heaven fright,
> For whose excrescence ill design'd,
> Nature must a new Center find,
> Learn here those humble steps to tread,
> Which to securer Glory lead.[1]

The third stanza is a compact repetition of the kind of association which Denham had given to Windsor. The hill is both femininely attractive—'see what a soft access and wide Lyes open to its grassy side'—and thoughtful in a gentlemanly way:

> See then how courteous it ascends,
> And all the way it rises bends;
> Not for it self the height does gain,
> But only strives to raise the Plain.

The reconciliation of hill and plain once again represents good government and deportment, only this time it is the government of Fairfax. If the private and domestic virtues are described in the third stanza, it is the public virtues of the hill

---

[1] Sylvester, ed. cit., p. 48: 'crump shoulders' of mountains; and Scot, *Philomythie*, sig. A2ᵛ, 'crumpshoulderd' of the world deformed from original circularity, with mention of Richard of Gloucester.

that are emphasized in the fourth, introduced by a simple pun on 'field'. Drayton had included usefulness as a landmark among the qualities of hills;[1] for Marvell this has the additional double reference to Fairfax's share in naval leadership,[2] and to his national duties. Sarbiewski had mentioned a fortress with its banner at the top of Bracciano's hill; and Marvell seems to have remembered the passage to the extent of verbal borrowing, though his adaptation is individual.[3] What is fact in Sarbiewski becomes conceit in Marvell: it is not the banner of Fairfax which causes fear to the invader, but the very disposition of the trees on the hill-top, a symbolic reminder of his military power.

> Upon its crest this Mountain grave
> A Plump of aged Trees does wave.
> No hostile hand durst ere invade
> With impious Steel the sacred Shade.

A well-known Spenserian simile had compared the helmet of a warrior to a hill bearing a plume of trees,[4] and in it Marvell seems to have noticed a special relevance to Fairfax, who had survived warfare inviolate, and now wished to maintain his privacy by preserving his protective trees unfelled.

> For something alwaies did appear
> Of the *great Masters* terrour there:
> And Men could hear his Armour still
> Ratling through all the Grove and Hill.

The 'raucosque silvarum fragor' of Sarbiewski has become an emblem of Fairfax's power.

In pastoral love-poetry, the incision made in a tree-trunk represents the incision of love in the heart.[5] With strict

[1] See *Poly-Olbion*, xiv. 125–30, *Britannia's Pastorals*, i. iii. 373; ii. v. 166.

[2] In 1650 Fairfax was appointed to the Council of State, which superintended both naval and civil affairs. (See E. E. Duncan-Jones, *The Times Literary Supplement*, 1955, p. 673.)

[3] Røstvig, op. cit., pp. 239–43. Cf. 'A displayd Banner from on hye, / Which to th'Imperiall force a terrour was' and Marvell's 'the *great Masters* terrour', the most convincing of the parallels suggested.

[4] See *Faerie Queene*, i. vii. 32; *Tamburlaine, Part II*, iv. iii. 115–20.

[5] See *Britannia's Pastorals*, ii. iv. 831–8; Herrick, 'To Groves' (*Hesperides*, no. 450, ed. cit., p. 169); Cowley, 'The Tree'.

consistency in transferring erotic conceits to the description of nature's love for man, Marvell shifted the image of the scarred heart to the trees themselves. Before Fairfax had engraved his wife's name on his grove, ' 'Twas writ already in their Heart'.

The final stanzas are a compressed collection of common conceits and emblematic associations, given some sort of originality by the coherence and orderliness of their presentation. The genius of the house which lives in a tree,[1] the tree which is a memorial of its master,[2] the tree felled in the wind because of rash aspiration, the breeze carrying love-messages, 'Groves of Pikes'[3] and 'Civick Garlands' are all combined in honour of one man and one place. Marvell's skill lies in the ordering and development of conceits rather than in their invention, and the last stanza is his contribution to the debate between hill and valley. In his Latin poem, 'Epigramma in Duos montes Amosclivum et Bilboreum. Farfacio',[4] one hill is wild and high, the other soft and gentle; and the two together represent the two sides of Fairfax's character, 'Asper in adversos, facilis cedentibus idem'. As God unites contraries in the natural world, so does the hero in his realm.

> Dissimilis Domino coiit Natura sub uno;
> Farfaciaque tremunt sub ditione pares.

In this poem, the hill on which stands a grove of trees is an example of nature's wit, of her own special resolution of opposites, just as Fairfax's character is another example of her sportful seriousness, on a human level.

> Nor he the Hills without the Groves,
> Nor Height but with Retirement loves.

---

[1] For sympathy of 'things vegetative' with man, see Britannia's Pastorals, II. ii. 611–12, Hesperides, nos. 421 and 724, 'To the Genius of his house' (ed. cit., pp. 158, 245).

[2] Cf. Ben Jonson, 'To Penshurst', 13–14, and Claudian, 'De sene Veronense'. For emblems of the over-abundant tree, see Alciati, Emblemata, lxxiii, Camerarius, Centuriae, I. x ('Neglecta juventus'), I. xiii ('Me copia perdit'). In Alciati, ccii, 'Picea', the growth of roots means offspring.

[3] Sylvester, ed. cit., p. 64, 'stand of Pikes', for the stiff bristles of wheat. See Alciati, I. xix, xlvii for family-shields or imprese hung on trees, 'The Trophees of one fertile Year'.　　　　　　　　　　　　　　　　　　　　　[4] Ed. cit., i. 55.

II

When Marvell came to organize his patron's landscape somewhat more ambitiously in his other estate-poem, 'Upon Appleton House, to my Lord *Fairfax*', it was again by reconciling opposing qualities, and by demonstrating multiplicity in unity. The controlling sense behind the poem is that Fairfax's 'little world commands the great'.[1] The estate is presented paradoxically as 'a Retreat from the world, as it is mans; into the world, as it is Gods'.[2] The greater world is annihilated, not by denying its values and characteristics, but by showing how they are included with completeness in the estate, which is presented as the realization of the poets' myths of imaginary places, Arcadia, the Bower of Bliss, Jerusalem, Elisium, and as the fulfilment of several fashionable paradoxes,

> As if it had by Natures cunning hand
> Bene choisely picked out from all the rest,
> And laid forth for ensample of the best.[3]

Comprehensiveness was a contemporary ideal in landscape-painting.[4] Nor was Marvell the only poet of the time to regard place or person in this way. Mildmay Fane's witty poem, 'To Sir John Wentworth, upon his Curiosities and Courteous entertainment at Summerly in Lovingland',[5] is built upon the same idea. Summerly contains all nature's wonders 'in Epitome' (a phrase popularized by Donne with reference to the beloved lady).

> The Fablers of old, I guess, might finde
> Some Objects t'help invention, but the minde
> Was sure Prophetick, for what ever is
> Describ'd for rare by them, 'twas meant by this.

---

[1] Edward Benlowes, *Theophila*, XIII. xx.

[2] Cowley, *Essays* (1668), 'Of Agriculture'.

[3] *Faerie Queene*, II. vi. 12. Francis Bacon described gardens as 'in small compass a model of universal nature made private'.

[4] See H. V. S. Ogden, op. cit., and with Margaret S. Ogden, *English Taste in Landscape in the Seventeenth Century* (1955). For contemporary statement, see Rémy Belleau, 'Le Pinceau'; Maurice Scève, *Le Microcosme* (1562), 111; Sylvester, ed. cit., p. 139; William Browne, *Britannia's Pastorals*, I. ii. 819–58; Henry Peacham, *Graphice* (1612), 'Of the Graces of Landtskip'

[5] *Otia Sacra*, p. 153.

The strangeness of the place is related to the variety of excellences included within such small scope, provided by the European 'Civility' of its owner.

> Now as contracted vertue doth excell
> In power and force, This seems a Miracle;
> Wherein all Travailers may truly say,
> They never saw so much in little way:
> And thence conclude their folly, that did steer
> To seek for that abroad, at home was neer
> In more perfection.

It was by using for his own ends the conventions associated
with different sorts of poem that Marvell suggested that he
found encompassed in the Appleton estate 'All that's made',
whether in nature or in art, 'a Monopolie of al the pleasures
and delights that are on earth, amassed togeather, to make a
dearth therof els-where'.[1] The themes related to country life
which he recalled and combined into a new whole included
the meditation on the superiority of the humble life to the life
of ambition,[2] the history and patriotic praise of a place,[3] the
enumeration of a day's activities in the country, with its *aubade*,
its morning-walk, and its account of nightfall,[4] the journey,[5]
the allegorical description of the interior garden, and the poem
of contemplation passing from one object to another with the
the purpose 'to know the Heavenly use of earthly things'.[6] All
these patterns of artifice are to be found within 'Upon Appleton
House', unified by a style whose core is the discovery of
resemblance between things apparently unlike, and between
different kinds of life, heroic and rustic, biblical and con-

---

[1] Henry Hawkins, *Partheneia Sacra*, p. 6, 'The Garden'.

[2] See M.-S. Røstvig, *The Happy Man*, for an account of the important seventeenth-
century poems on this theme.

[3] See William Warner, *Albions England*; Drayton, *Poly-Olbion*.

[4] See S. R. Watson, 'Milton's Ideal Day: Its Development as a Pastoral Theme',
P.M.L.A. lxvii (1942), 404-20.

[5] See R. A. Aubin, *Topographical Poetry in XVIII-Century England* (New York,
1936), chaps. i, vii, and bibliography.

[6] From a poem by Fairfax himself, in Bodleian MS. Fairfax 40, p. 485. Cf. John
Hagthorpe, *Divine Meditations* (1622); Ann Bradstreet, *The Tenth Muse* (1650), 'Con-
templations'; Benlowes, *Theophila*, xii, xiii; Saint Amant, *Œuvres Poètiques* (1629),
'Le Contemplateur'; Sarbiewski, *Lyricorum libri IV*, ed. cit., third epode, p. 212.

temporary, exotic and local, small and great, erotic and ascetic, pious and profane. Reason is combined with the irrational, magic with the mundane, and the categories of painting, drama, and science are shown to have some relevance to the Fairfax demesnes. There is not another place-poem of the same length from the seventeenth century which has as its intention the display of such varieties.

There is still another inclusive device, which Du Bartas used. His rural scene was not 'better than' classical gardens (a pattern of comparison common from Spenser to Milton),[1] but was identified with them:

> The silver Brooke his sweetest *Hypocrasse*.

And Sylvester added his local version:

> Bee *Hadley Pond* my *Sea: Lambesbourne* my Thames;
> *Lambourne* my *London*: Kennet's silver streames
> My fruitful *Nile*.

Marvell's poem is distinctive in the resolution with which he applied one category to everything, especially the military metaphor, with its special appropriateness to the retired general, Fairfax. Often in his use of this conceit he seems to be recollecting rather than inventing, as though he had kept a commonplace book during his residence at Nun Appleton and were referring to it during the composition of his poetry. Perhaps this was no more than an excellent memory. In stanzas xxxvi and xliv morality, landscape, and fortification are identified. The 'five imaginary Forts' which defend his garden may seem a frivolous retreat from real warfare, but they are also symbols of his preference for interior warfare, the battle of mind and senses. In making the senses 'five Bastions' he was not inventing a conceit, but choosing a fashionable one which had particular relevance to his patron; for Fairfax had been Lord Warden of the Cinque Ports during 1650 and 1651.[2]

One way of praising a country life is to eliminate its rivals as they crowd for an entrance, and this is the method commonly

---

[1] See for example, *Faerie Queene*, II. xii. 52, *Paradise Lost*, iv. 264–85.
[2] See E. E. Duncan-Jones in the letter already cited.

used by the Elizabethan poets. Sidney wrote one stanza of three in his poem 'O sweete woods, the delight of solitarines'[1] on this principle, with no less than eleven negatives in it. Du Bartas and Ben Jonson followed the same course.[2] Yet there was another way besides elimination, and that was comprehension, by showing a correspondence between the state of the garden and the outer world. 'Fair trees' shade is enough fortification.'[3]

> How safe, methinks, and strong, behind
> These Trees have I incamp'd my Mind.[4]

Du Bartas had his military conceits, 'The Fields of Corne, as Fields of Combat', 'Ranks of Trees, as Ranks of Souldiers'. Battles are fought with 'Beast, Bird, or Fish',[5] The crested Cock sings *Hunt is up*', the 'happie Rusticks weale' is 'as a Common-weale', with its own small sea watering its meadows. Fane's poem to Wentworth has also its garden commonwealth and its life-guard trees. According to William Lawson in *A New Orchard and Garden* (1623), the topiarists' art was affected by this fancy, and trees were shaped to resemble soldiers or greyhounds following hare and deer. 'This kinde of hunting shal not waste your corne, nor much your coyne.'[6]

Fairfax's gardens too had been laid out 'in sport', and the extent of their soldiery was measurable in bee-terms. The course of the day begins when 'the Morning Ray' hangs out its colours. Heaven and earth are in agreement: nothing in the

---

[1] *Arcadia* (1593), ed. Feuillerat (Cambridge, 1922), p. 237.
[2] See Sylvester, ed. cit., pp. 69–71; *Ben Jonson*, ed. Herford and Simpson, viii. 93, 96: 'To Penshurst', 'To Sir Robert Wroth'.
[3] Sidney, op. cit., p. 237.
[4] Marvell, st. lxxvi. Cf. Horace, *Odes*, I. xxii. 1–4, rendered by Roscommon (1666):

> Vertue, Dear Friend, needs no Defence,
> No Arms but its own Innocence.

[5] See Juvenal, *Satires*, iv. 68–69, for the willingness of creatures to be killed, and cf. Jonson, 'To Penshurst' on 'The painted partrich'. See *Georgics*, ii. 142–4, for comparison of corn to soldiers, and cf. with the abundance of military conceits in *Partheneia Sacra*. For comparison of hunt to warfare, see Turbervile, *The Booke of Faulconrie* (1575), 'In commendation of Hawking' and Turbervile, *The Noble Arte of Venerie or Hunting* (1575). 'George Gascoigne, in the commendation of the noble Arte of Venerie'.
[6] P. 55.

landscape is not militarized. Even 'the vigilant *Patroul* / Of Stars walks round about the *Pole*', But if the introduction to the garden is a playful one, the tone is not sustained. There is an irony about its structure, for it lies within a larger and molested garden, 'that dear and happy Isle / The Garden of the World ere while', which has become 'The Wast'. So the existence of all this useless militarism in the Fairfax garden has a poignancy about it, and is accompanied by a wish, enclosed in a pun, that 'Ord'nance Plant' should be replaced by the 'tender Plants' of the hothouse. Predecessors had used the 'magazeen' conceit for the plenty of the earth, but without much point. It needed Marvell to enliven it by giving it relevant social implications.

> The Nursery of all things green
> Was then the only *Magazeen*.

Soldiery is maintained in the stanzas describing the mowing of the fields. The bee had somewhat merrily beat 'the *Dian*'; the parent-rail more sombrely rings a death-knell.

> Death-Trumpets creak in such a Note,
> And 'tis the *Sourdine* in their Throat.

The warfare is changed, it is no longer contemporary, but the warfare of the Israelites marching to the Promised Land, of Antony with the Romans.[1]

Still another battle is waged at the end of the poem, which is united with the beginning by making Maria's ambush of hearts[2] counteract the use of persuasive force by the nuns.[3] Their defeat has been presented in heroic terms belonging to the romantic epic. They were associated with the illusory castles of *Gerusalemme Liberata*, possibly in compliment to an earlier Fairfax who had translated Tasso into English.[4] Even this allusion would have an irony about it which would be

---

[1] The Israelites appear in stanzas xlix, li, Alexander in liv, Antony in lv, with its references to 'Short Pyramids of Hay' resembling Roman burial-mounds.
[2] Stanza lxxxx.
[3] Stanzas xiv, xxiv, xxvi, xxxi, xxxii.
[4] Edward Fairfax, *Godfrey of Bulloigne* (1600).

more readily apprehended by the contemporary reader. For Spenser's Bower of Bliss was destroyed in the end, and Tasso's magical garden disappeared, as Marvell recalls in stanza xxxiiii:

Thenceforth (as when th'Inchantment ends
The Castle vanishes or rends)
The wasting Cloister with the rest
Was in one instant dispossest.

Instead, the Appleton estate 'To *Fairfax* fel as by Escheat'; the garden was not demolished, but repossessed by one whose magic was lawful. So the remarkable effects which the presence of Maria has on the garden possess particular significance within this contemporary romantic tale, in contrast to the black magic with which the poem begins; for the nuns had said that Isabel Thwaites, Maria's ancestress, would be like the Virgin Mary, and that her virtue would increase 'Till Miracles it work at last'. It is true that there are not many stanzas in the poem which recall the romantic epic in their construction. Yet the few that there are (lxxxviii, lxxxiv, lxxxxv, and lxxxxvi, for example) have Maria and her place of enchantment as their centre. The making of the Appleton estate into a romantic retirement also adds irony to Fairfax's own possession of it. Such a place is almost invariably a place of temptation to the noble knight; but for this soldier it is a place of meditation.

III

Travel, like affairs of state, is both denied and included in the garden. For Fairfax 'in those half-dry Trenches, spann'd, / Pow'r which the Ocean might command'. The 'Abbyss' of 'that unfathomable Grass' is not defined clearly at first as the sea, though its 'Precipices' give the hint. In stanza xlviii the conceit is magnificently continued, with a certain resemblance to a stanza in a country-poem by Wotton, which suggests that Marvell had lately been reading Walton's *The Compleat Angler* (1653) in which it appeared. Wotton had renounced the gems of 'the diving Negro' for the pearls which 'the dewy morn /

Congeals upon each little spire of grasse'. Marvell sees 'Men through this Meadow Dive' and 'bring up Flow'rs so to be seen, / And prove they've at the Bottom been'.

Then the sea of the 'Marriners' turns into the sea of the Hebrew children. The astute seventeenth-century reader would perhaps be aware of a negation in his 'green Sea' of the Red Sea, not only as the miraculous crossing-place of the Israelites, but also as the stretch of water which Claudian had put in opposition to lake Benacus in his poem on the old man of Verona.

> *Verona* he doth for the *Indies* take,
> And for the *red sea* counts *Benacus'* lake.[1]

In the fifty-fifth stanza, there is a transition from sea to river, but to a river dried up by the summer sun. The landscape has been turned topsy-turvy by the alteration of the seasons, the real identity of things and places is confused, and so can only be defined in a paradox.

> When after this 'tis pil'd in Cocks,
> Like a calm Sea it shews the Rocks:
> We wondring in the River near
> How Boats among them safely steer.

In more than one Elizabethan play, an image which appears at first only figuratively becomes fact as the action proceeds.[2] In the same way, the imaginary flood in this poem becomes a real flood, when '*Denton* sets ope its *Cataracts*', and the Meadow becomes '(What it but seem'd before) a Sea'.[3] Deucalion's deluge and Noah's repeat themselves within Fairfax's bounds. In 'retiring from the Flood' in stanza lxi, Marvell at once maintains the classical theme of country-life *versus* travel, and christianizes Ovid,[4] by entering 'This yet green, yet growing Ark'. Donne had written of the ark as 'that floating park' in which all the creatures were housed.[5] By the change of a letter in one

---

[1] *Works of Henry Vaughan*, ed. L. C. Martin, p. 655.
[2] Cf. the dramatic anticipation in stanza xxxiii.
[3] Cf. Margaret Cavendish, *Poems and Fancies* (1653), p. 146, 'The Sea similized to Meadows and Pastures'.   [4] See *Metamorphoses*, i. 291–312.
[5] *The Progresse of the Soule*, iii. Cf. Sylvester, ed. cit., pp. 238, 244.

of Donne's rhyming-words ('Embark', 'park'), Marvell trans-
ported another meaning into it, the meaning enclosed in Lovelace's line, 'Imbark thee in the Lawrell tree'.[1] By entering the
wood, the poet becomes both the patriarch among the trees
and a tree himself.

> But I, retiring from the Flood,
> Take Sanctuary in the Wood;
> And, while it lasts, my self imbark
> In this yet green, yet growing Ark.

It seems hardly to be a coincidence that the image which
Cowley chose for the definition of true wit is an image selected
by Marvell to suggest both order and profusion in the landscape.

> As in the *Ark*, joyn'd without force or strife,
> All *Creatures* dwelt; all *Creatures* that had *Life*.[2]

Besides this, the military analogy is given a new application,
carrying an impression of super-abundance: in the forest-ark
the creatures appear 'in Armies, not in Paires'.

The image of water recurs in the seventy-ninth stanza, which
Mr. Eliot has included among his special commendations.

> For now the Waves are fal'n and dry'd,
> And now the Meadows fresher dy'd;
> Whose Grass, with moister colour dasht,
> Seems as green Silks but newly washt.

It is no doubt true that in this section of the poem Marvell is
recalling St. Amant's 'La Solitude' and Théophile's 'La Maison
de Sylvie'.[3] Yet the kind of transformation which takes place
in the landscape is peculiar to Marvell: the river is turned into
an animal, and man into earth and river. The river is a serpent,
not only in shape, but as the modest creature of an unfallen
paradise. Donne's 'Twickenham Garden' had been marred by
its evil post-lapsarian presence.

---

[1] 'Aramantha. A Pastorall', 274.
[2] *Miscellanies* (1668), p. 4, 'Ode. Of Wit'.
[3] See Ruth Wallerstein, *Seventeenth-Century Poetic* (1950), chap. ix, on connexions
with St. Amant.

And that this place may thoroughly be thought
True Paradise, I have the serpent brought.[1]

Marvell's river is a reversal of this: it is 'our little *Nile*' whose existence denies the 'serpent of old Nile', Cleopatra and all that she represents, heroic and illicit love, ambition, discontent with limitations and exotic wanderings; for its folds are 'wanton harmless', and its back is a '*Chrystal Mirrour*', just as Maria herself is 'Chrystal-pure'.

The eighty-first stanza is another exercise in transformation. The poet becomes a river-god, with a posture reminiscent of Renaissance statuary and illustrations. Yet he is even closer to the natural state than to myth. His side is 'a Bank unto the Tide', and the 'glissant pas' of poetic tradition becomes 'my sliding Foot'. It is the fish who play poet, as they 'twang' at his 'Lines', while in his stillness and concentration as an angler he is less elevated in the scale of nature than they, by an act of voluntary humility, not unmixed with amusement.

The poem's journey ends when the salmon-fishers bring their boats up from the river,

> And, like *Antipodes* in Shoes,
> Have shod their *Heads* in their *Canoos*.

The wit of this final stanza, which has earned Mr. Eliot's disapproval, is an extension of more than one contemporary literary joke. A poem that was full of creatures suspended between two elements would conclude fitly with the mention of 'rational *Amphibii*', oddly resembling that other amphibian, the tortoise, with which the poem had begun. Du Bartas, remembering Pliny, had described the large Arabian tortoise from which a boat might be made.

> But of one *Tortoise*, when he list to float,
> Th'*Arabian* Fisher-man can make a Boat;
> And one such Shell, him in the stead doth stand
> Of Hulk at Sea, and of a House on land.[2]

---

[1] 'Songs and Sonets' (1633) in *The Poems of John Donne*, ed. H. J. C. Grierson, (Clarendon Press, Oxford, 1912, 2 vols.), i. 28.

[2] Sylvester, ed. cit., p. 93. Philemon Holland's *Pliny*, IX. x (1634 ed., i. 241) runs: 'There be found Tortoises in the Indian sea so great, that one only shel of them is

Marvell took the notion a stage farther and transformed fishers into tortoises. The world consists of one shell within another: over all is 'the dark *Hemisphere*', and within are men and animals similarly housed and enclosed.

The 'Antipodes, such as walke with their feet against ours'[1] became useful metaphorically to describe such wonders as a hall of mirrors, turning the world awry:

> Nay, to reverse the miracle, with ease
> We are become our own Antipodes.[2]

So the coming of night distorts the order of the universe, making men and things seem what they are not; and yet this very semblance is the assertion of another kind of order, in which great is contained in little. The inhabitants of the Appleton estate need not go *alio . . . sub sole* (the Virgilian phrase rendered 'their Antipodes' by Cowley)[3] to find delight and profusion. There is a time of day when even the oddest miracles of the ends of the earth are comprehended within their own boundaries.

IV

When Maria Fairfax walked by the water she was not subject to it, but performed miracles by her very presence. There was hardly a garden in Tudor poetry without some lady central to it, either Elizabeth or some more private person, or Venus, or Lady Nature herself. Sometimes her features were compared to the universe, sometimes she was given magic powers over it. In one poem 'there is a garden in her face', in another her robes are a cosmic image, in another she draws the admiration

sufficient for the roufe of a dwelling house. And among the Islands principally in the Red sea, they use Tortoise shells ordinarily for boats and wherries upon the water'. Z. Heyns, *Emblemata Moralia* (Rotterdam, 1625), III, fols. 6ᵛ–7ʳ, 'Vivitur parva bene', illustrates this lore.

[1] Quoted from Lactantius, *Institutes*, III. xxiv, by Bishop Wilkins, *A Discourse concerning A New World & Another Planet* (1640), pp. 7–8. Cf. Augustine, *Of the Citie of God*, XVI. ix.

[2] *Parnassus Biceps* (1656), p. 32. Cf. Poole, *English Parnassus* (1657), p. 285, 'Evening': 'The morning of the Antipodes'.

[3] *The Works of Mr. Abraham Cowley* (1668), p. 106, 'A Translation out of Virgil' from *Georgics* ii. 511–12, on the country life versus travel.

of the creatures, enchanting them, making them perform the impossible. Sometimes she is offered gifts from the world's abundance by her lover. Seldom is the lord of nature treated so variedly as the lady (though the behaviour of the wood-creatures towards Marvell, and his rustic cope, are traditional patterns). In Maria true womanhood is presented, in opposition to the evil power over nature and people typified in the nuns.

> 'Tis *She* that to these Gardens gave
> That wondrous Beauty which they have;
>
> . . . . .
>
> She yet more Pure, Sweet, Streight, and Fair,
> Then Gardens, Woods, Meads, Rivers are.

She is superior to the sonneteers' ladies, to Elizabeth, to the nuns, even to the Catholic Queen of Heaven, for 'all *Virgins* She preceds'.[1] Maria is the Lady of the Evening, and is given associations which Collins reserved for Eve herself a century later: she is chaste, retiring, modest. As night falls on the river, Marvell imagines the '*Eben Shuts*' of the shadows to be closing upon it, '*Eben*' suggesting both the colour of the shadows themselves, and the trees by the water's edge which cast them, darkened to look like exotic ebony by the disappearance of the sun. In his poem 'La Solitude', the contemporary French poet Théophile de Viau had created a river-nymph to open the crystal door of the water.[2] The 'Shuts' or shutters of this poem suggest the same kind of odd transformation of the river into a house, closing up in the evening.

> So when the Shadows laid asleep
> From underneath these Banks do creep,
> And on the River as it flows
> With *Eben Shuts* begin to close;

---

[1] The poem may be, among other things, a literary riposte to contemporary praise of the Virgin Mary, such as there is in *Partheneia Sacra*.

[2] *Œuvres Complètes*, ed. Alleaume (Paris, 1856), i. 176:

> De ceste source une Naiade,
> Tous les soirs ouvre le portail,
> De sa demeure de crystal,
> Et nous chante une sérénade.

> The modest *Halcyon* comes in sight,
> Flying betwixt the Day and Night;
> And such an horror calm and dumb,
> *Admiring Nature* does benum.

In this stanza the connective 'so' might be merely a loose introductory word; but it is the initiation of a simile. Maria resembles some of the most mysterious creatures in her own landscape. Her affinities are with the halcyon and the comet, belonging to the middle-regions, participating both in earth and in heaven.

Other miraculous birds had caused wonder before Marvell's; other poets used similar words:

> Let me stand numb'd with wonder, never came
> So strong amazement on astonish'd eie
> As this, this measureles pure Raritie.[1]

'Benum' was used precisely by Marvell with a double reference. The landscape, regarded anthropomorphically, was experiencing the ecstasy of a trance at the appearance of the blessed lady. To the eye, it had become still, fixed in a solid state. The two meanings are held together, the human and the scientific, since the external appearance of things is an emblem of inner significances. These two kinds of meaning are interfused in the following stanza also.

> The viscous Air, wheres'ere She fly,
> Follows and sucks her Azure dy;
> The gellying Stream compacts below,
> If it might fix her shadow so;
> The stupid Fishes hang, as plain
> As *Flies* in *Chrystal* overt'ane;
> And Men the silent *Scene* assist,
> Charm'd with the *Saphir-winged Mist*.

Here the contemporary vocabulary of magnetism is interwoven with a traditional literary imagery, derived from the classical

---

[1] In Robert Chester, *Loves Martyr*, Marston's accompanying poem on the phoenix and the turtle.

epigrammatists. It is necessary not only to say that the bird gives its colour to the evening sky, but to explain this as a scientific process. A passage in Sir Thomas Browne's *Vulgar Errors* throws light on the matter:

Another way of their attraction is also delivered; that is, by a tenuous emanation or continued effluvium, which after some distance retracteth into it self; as is observable in drops of Syrups, Oyl and seminal Viscosities, which spun at length, retire into their former dimensions. Now these effluviums advancing from the body of the Electrick, in their return do carry back to bodies whereon they have laid hold within the Sphere or Circle of their continuities; and these they do not onley attract, but with their viscous arms hold fast for a good while after.[1]

Besides the adjective 'viscous', the verb 'to suck' was used technically in descriptions of magnetism: the spirit of iron was thought to be sucked by the loadstone.[2] So the air attracted the colour of the halcyon to itself.

Other poets before Marvell had described birds' shadows on the surface of the water.

But as the Raven late, he next sends out
The damaske coloured Dove, his nimble Scout,
Which thrils the thin Ayre, and his pyneons plyes,
That like to lightning, glyding through the Skyes,
His sundry coloured feathers by the Sunne,
As his swift shadow on the Lake doth runne,
Causeth a twinckling both at hand and farre,
Like that we call the shooting of a Starre.[3]

Drayton's image is predominantly a visual one; but by introducing a semblance of cause and effect, Marvell produced a conceit which at once presents a facet of the landscape, the coming of stillness and darkness over the water as the bird flies

---

[1] *Enquiries into Vulgar and Common Errors*, II. iv.
[2] See Oswald Crollius, *Philosophy Reformed & Improved* (1657), translated by H. Pinnell, p. 45. In William Cartwright, 'The Gnat' (ed. cit., p. 478), 'suck' is used of the action of jet upon straws.
[3] Drayton, *Noah's Floud*, in *Complete Works*, ed. J. W. Hebel, iii. 349.

across, and a value-judgement, the extreme worth of the bird, so that even the catching of its shadow is important. The halcyon has brought night with it, and not merely accompanied it.

One of the most notable features of this poem is its presentation of transitional states and changes in the face of things. Marvell himself was attempting to fix shadows, to make something permanent of impermanence; and this twilight passage is the climax of that part of the poem's meaning. Like Marvell, Herrick was fascinated by 'doubtful Twi-light', by the concealment of one thing within another. There are certain resemblances between this passage and 'The Lilly in a Christal'.[1] Behind them lie some lines from the Latin poets, and a kind of descriptiveness to be found in the romances. The power of the lady operates not in the full blaze of day, but in the half-light which stands for mystery; the beauty of things consists not only in their order, but in the enfolding of one kind of excellence within another. The lily is 'More faire in this transparent case, / Then when it grew alone; / And had but single grace.' The halcyon hovering over 'The stupid Fishes' brings about the fulfilment of their beauty as they are fixed in the crystal water. The sun had first 'In blushing Clouds' concealed 'his Head'; the windows of the river were closed, and now the fish are entombed; and these successive veilings of the landscape suggest first Maria's modesty, and then the power of her goodness. In Herrick's poem the 'Scean' was the veil or curtain (a relatively new meaning of the word),[2] 'cast over, / To juggle with the sense'. Though an awareness of the deceptiveness of twilight is not absent from Marvell's lines, his emphasis lies rather on the wonder aroused both in the creatures and in the men who are spectators (who 'assist' in the Latin root-sense of the word). 'Charm'd' bears the treble sense of delight, hypnotization by a spell, and the ecstasy which is the culmination of an act of contemplation.[3]

---

[1] *Hesperides*, no. 193 (ed. cit., p. 75).

[2] *N.E.D.* records the first use in 1638, with associations with the meaning 'scenery', applied to the stage.

[3] See Sir George McKenzie, *Religio Stoici* (1665): 'Contemplation does often drive

'The *Saphir-winged Mist*' is more than an exquisite pictorial periphrasis for the halcyon, of the same kind as Habington's 'feather'd Musicke' and Lovelace's 'wing'd musick of the ayre'. Even these phrases are attempts to describe the immateriality of a creature; but Marvell's phrase carries further suggestions. Belief in daimons of the elements during the Renaissance was associated with the idea that the impalpable spirit must take a less spiritual form in order to live and communicate its being. And some spirits were believed to clothe themselves in air.[1] The emblematic associations of air may be found in *Partheneia Sacra*; the rainbow is compared to the Virgin Mary, and each of its colours is deciphered.

She had thirdly the coulour of the Hyacinth; which *she* tooke, as from the ayre; since al *her* conversation was in the ayre, as it were, abstracted from the earth, or terrene cogitations; *she* was wholy as the *Bird of Paradise*, which hath no feet to touch the earth with; & from the time that her Sonne ascended to heaven, from the mount Olivet, she could do nothing but cast up her eyes thitherwards, and so powerfully perhaps contracted that coulour, through the vehemencie of her attention, and application to that object, til her *Assumption* haply, when *she* left it by the way in her Bow, to remayne for ever, as a signe of her puritie.[2]

Among weather-poems of the seventeenth century, the theme of congelation was not unpopular.[3] It was a subject which might produce a profusion of clumsy conceits; but like the Nun Appleton kingfisher and the girl whom it typified Marvell refined upon the landscape which he inherited. He preserved the image of the solidifying of the water, but reduced its grotesqueness. In his poem, crystal is both substance and symbol, and his successive definitions of it on one level add to its richness at another level of significance. Isabel Thwaites in the

our souls into extasies, and is so charming, that it may be rather said to ravish then please'; Habington, *Castara* (1634), iii, 'Recogitabo tibi omnes animos meos'; Lovelace, 'Aramantha. A Pastorall', 165.

[1] R. Bassett, *Curiosities, or The Cabinet of Nature* (1637), p. 113, 'Of Apparitions in the Aire', compares them to pigeons' feathers, taffeta, and the rainbow in their changes of colour. [2] ix, 'The Iris', p. 98.

[3] For example, John Heath, *Two Centuries of Epigrams* (1610), 'De gelu diutinu. Ann. Dom. 1607'; William Cartwright, 'On the great Frost, 1634'.

company of the nuns is 'Like Chrystal pure with Cotton warm'. The compliments offered her are in the manner of a rustic wooing, with its combination of rich substances to tempt the maiden or praise her person. In the eightieth stanza, 'Chrystal' is set in another context, pastoral and mythological: it describes the quality of the river in which all things are mirrored. Ice was 'water Chrystaliz'd' for the seventeenth century;[1] and in the *Greek Anthology* ice had enclosed children and animals.[2] These associations lie behind the '*Flies* in *Chrystal* overt'ane' of stanza lxxxv. Yet there is a further reason, a moral one, for the illusory crystallization of the water, apart from the cold of winter. This lies in the nature of the lady herself, whose influence causes refinement of the elements.[3] Crystal was to Marvell's contemporaries an emblem of the purity and durability of true faith; it was the untainted substance left after the earth had been tried by fire.[4] So it might represent either perfection in temporal life, or the life after death.[5] The passing of Maria through the evening is like the process of a comet, bringing not baleful news and trouble, the destructive scorching of the earth which the comet traditionally carried, but a flame which purifies because it is heavenly. So the calm and delicate beauty of the dusk is a symbol of the purifying power of Maria Fairfax over all creatures. '*Nature* is wholly *vitrifi'd.*'

> Nothing could make the River be
> So Chrystal-pure but only *She*.

---

[1] Joshua Poole, *English Parnassus* (1657), 'Ice'.

[2] vii. 542; ix. 56, on a boy beheaded by ice (Hutton, op. cit., records thirty-two Renaissance versions and imitations); cf. Martial, iv. 18. Also *Greek Anthology*, ix. 244, on frozen deer. In England, see William Browne, 'On one drowned in the snow', in *Wits Recreations* (1640) and *Parnassus Biceps* (1656); Thomas Jordan, *Poetical Varieties* (1637), 'An Elegie on the death of a Male-child drown'd in Ice'.

[3] Drayton, ed. cit., ii. 337, '*Idea*', liii: 'Thy crystall streame refined by her Eyes'.

[4] T. Palfreyman, *The Treatise of Heavenly Philosophie* (1578), pp. 798–9: 'Like as the Christall stone is made of the most cleare and faire water, and by continuaunce of time congeled into a durable and harde substance: even so, that true faith, whiche is annexed and knit (as it ought) unto holie baptisme, is brought to perfection by long continuance of time, and patient bearing of adversities.'

[5] See Thomas Philipott, *Poems* (1646), ed. L. C. Martin (Liverpool Reprints, no. 4, 1950), p. 54, 'On thought of our Resurrection'; Vaughan, *Silex Scintillans*, 'L'Envoy'.

V

Lately the history of the ideal of self-containedness as it is expressed in seventeenth-century poetry has been traced in considerable detail. It is with a version of this theme that Marvell's poem opens. Yet though his theme is essentially an Horatian one, no style could be less classical at first sight than his. There is paradox not only in his statement, but in his style itself in relation to his subject. For the great man the small estate is most appropriate; yet humility is praised in a bombastic manner whose swellings in the seventh stanza Mr. Eliot found so distasteful. Still, the advance from one single self-coherent stanza to another keeps such a style in order, in an epigrammatic way, each stanza beginning in an undemanding tone, but working up to a witty climax. And Marvell had contemporary theory with him (from Robortello, writing in 1548, to Thomas Pecke in his *Parnassi Puerperium* of 1659)[1] in making his poem a tissue of epigrams. Moreover, his compression of meaning is itself a decorous expression of the character of Fairfax, preventing the poem from becoming a 'hollow Palace' full of empty sound, like so many Elizabethan complimentary poems. It would have been an insult to treat of Fairfax as of Tamburlaine, 'That thinks by Breadth the World t'unite', in a style which would be a concession to the most hyperbolic romantic heroism, but would demand no brainwork.

The argument pursued by Marvell is that a man should live in a palace that is suitable to his status; yet that the famous live best in humble conditions. Paradox and decorum are interwoven, for example, in the eighth stanza, where the first four lines emphasize the first category, and the last four the second.

The suggestion of paradox is not absent from classical poems on the same subject. Horace wrote of the man who owns wealth excessive to his needs,[2] but without the kind of wit supplied to the idea by Marvell. Yet it is possible that Marvell was recollecting not only classical ideas but particular lines

---

[1] See W. Lee Ustick and Hoyt H. Hudson, 'Wit, "Mixt Wit" and the Bee in Amber', *Huntingdon Library Bulletin*, viii (1935), 103–30.

[2] *Epistles* I. x; *Satires*, i.

from his favourite Latin poets, finding in them a doubleness of reference not present in the original. So the fourth stanza may have something in it of the passage from the *Aeneid* (vi. 360 ff.) in which the hero stoops to enter a cottage-door, or of Horace's injunction, *Fuge magna: licet sub paupere tecto reges?*[1] There is elaboration upon another classical recollection in the sixth stanza, with its conceit of the expansion of a square into a circle. Marvell was not the first to meditate upon this impossibility. (Margaret Cavendish, the Duchess of Newcastle, has a poem entitled 'The *Circle* of the *Brain* cannot be *squared*'.)[2] In the categories of '*holy Mathematicks*' the circle stands for eternity, and the square for 'a constant minded man'.[3] It is only the man who lives a holy life who may resolve the ancient paradox, by combining temporal with eternal goodness, and by making any sort of architecture fit through his excellence of character. Square contains circle when an earthly house contains an eternal being. It is upon this idea that Marvell expands so extravagantly in the following stanza, vii, in which 'the *Square* grows *Spherical*'. Yet it might have stopped at the sixth stanza if Horace had not written the line *Diruit, aedificat, mutat quadrata rotundis*, of house-building.[4] Marvell set himself to find the one instance where such a transformation from square to circle is not an objectionable result of pride.

The moral significance of the place, if it does not already lurk in the word 'sober' in the first line, becomes more apparent as the poem unfolds. William Habington had in his *Castara* (1634) combined the Christian *memento mori* with the Horatian themes of warning against the ambition which travels too widely or builds too high. (The architectural theme is a common one in his more reflective poems.)

> Great Statist! tis your doome
> Though your designes swell high, and wide
> To be contracted in a tombe![5]

[1] *Epistles*, I. x. 32.
[2] *Poems and Fancies* (1653), p. 47.
[3] Puttenham, *The Arte of English Poesie*, II. xii, 'Of the square'.
[4] *Epistles*, I. i. 100.
[5] *Solum mihi est sepulchrum.*

This is the thought in Marvell's third stanza, 'What need of all this Marble Crust / T'impark the wanton Mote of Dust?' and the fourth intensifies the meditative tone. And in the fifth stanza, in praise of the 'dwarfish Confines', the 'Bee-like Cell' of the Fairfaxes, there is a cunning combination of pious and classical reflection with insect-limitation.

VI

Though adumbrations of the verse-meditation are present in 'Upon Appleton House' from the beginning, it is with the consideration of the 'Sanctuary in the Wood' that it becomes more conspicuous. The 'double Wood' has a special significance for the Fairfax family: it is an *imprese* of their fortunes, reminiscent of that common Renaissance emblem of harmony between trees representing faithful friendship or marriage.[1]

> The double Wood of ancient Stocks
> Link'd in so thick, an Union locks,
> It like two *Pedigrees* appears,
> On one hand *Fairfax*, th'other *Veres*.

The last four lines are entirely ambiguous, referring both to the united families and to the trees themselves. Jonson, in 'To Penshurst', had referred to a tree planted to represent the life of the hero Sidney; Marvell takes some lines from Claudian on the old man of Verona to clinch his stanza. 'A neighbouring Wood born with himself he sees / And loves his old contemporary Trees'[2] becomes

> And, as they Natures Cradle deckt,
> Will in green Age her Hearse expect.

The trees which in Claudian are only parallel in age with man are made to serve his necessities by Marvell, the necessities accompanying birth and death. The imprecise phrase 'Natures Cradle', while it refers primarily to the beginning of human

---

[1] See Alciati, clix; Camerarius, I. xl; and *Britannia's Pastorals*, II. iv. 652–7.
[2] Rendered by Cowley, op. cit., p. 136.

life, has a subsidiary reference to the early life of the world. Like Vaughan's creatures,[1] Marvell's trees are awaiting the redemption of the universe; their 'green Age' suggests hope of the end of time as well as their comparative youthfulness in relation to man's brief life, at the end of which they provide coffin and mourning-boughs. They are emblems both of the life of action ('many fell in War') and of the contemplative life ('Yet more to Heaven shooting are').

To describe the woodland temple of which the poet is priest is Marvell's next object. Like Astragon's Temple of Sorrow in Davenant's poem *Gondibert*, it 'seem'd the Palace of Eternal Night' with only one lamp inside, and the poet is given a robe like Astragon's mantle, 'Where Natures story was in Colours wrought'.[2] Though the 'artificial night' of the forest was commonplace to contemporary poetic landscape, Marvell presents it as though he were the first to think of it, as the climax of a stanza in which the mystery of the wood is predominant.

> When first the Eye this Forrest sees
> It seems indeed as Wood not *Trees*:
> As if their Neighbourhood so old
> To one great Trunk them all did mold.
> There the huge Bulk takes place, as ment
> To thrust up a *Fifth Element*;
> And stretches still so closely wedg'd
> As if the Night within were hedg'd.

The wood holds up the crystalline heavens, the '*Fifth Element*', and within is the vastness of the night skies. In some verses by James Howell, 'Before the Second Part of Dodona's Grove',[3] he had described the sight of mist covering the forest, so 'That the whole *Grove* appeer'd as one great *log*', probably in recollection of the Virgilian line, *namque uno ingentem tollit de caespite silvam*. So Marvell's trees are moulded 'To one great Trunk'.

The next magnificent stanza, lxiv, it has been shown, stems

---

[1] See 'The Seed growing secretly' and 'And do they so?'
[2] VI. xii, and lxxvi.
[3] *Dodona's Grove, or The Vocall Forest* (1640–50).

PLATE XIV

5

III.
PROSPICIEN-
TE DEO.

Si faueat cœlum, benè surculus arbore crescet:
Si faueat numen, tu quoq; magnus eris.

B   *Mul-*

Joachim Camerarius, *Symbolorum et Emblematum Centuriae* [1st edition], 1, iii,
Nuremberg, 1590

PLATE XV

A SHADIE Wood, pourtraiƈted to the ſight,
With vncouth pathes, and hidden waies vnknowne:
Reſembling *CHAOS*, or the hideous night,
Or thoſe ſad Groues, by banke of *ACHERON*
With banefull *Ewe*, and *Ebon* overgrowne:
  Whoſe thickeſt boughes, and inmoſt entries are
  Not peirceable, to power of any ſtarre.

Thy Impreſe *SILVIVS*, late I did deviſe,
To warne the what (if not) thou oughtſt to be,
Thus inward cloſe, vnſearch'd with outward eies,
With thouſand angles, light ſhould never ſee:
For fooles that moſt are open-hearted free,
  Vnto the world, their weakenes doe bewray,
  And to the net, the firſt themſelues betray.

Henry Peacham, *Minerva Britanna*, London, 1612

from a Latin poem by Benlowes,[1] but in such a way that
Marvell seems to have really seen what Benlowes had left
rather colourless. The rustic chapel had become a poetic
commonplace. Birds are called 'priests with their houses in the
trees' in Fane's Latin poem, 'Ad Amicum, de Vita Beata'. In
1622 there had appeared Godfrey Goodman's *The Creatures
Praising God*, a surprising devotional disquisition which defends
as true the notion that the creatures have their own worship
and sacraments. Yet credit must go to Benlowes for expanding
the analogies between wood and temple. In his adaptation,
Marvell added a suggestion of pre-Christian religion in '*Corinthean Porticoes*', as well as the tell-tale phrase, 'as loose an order',
betraying the nature of his own aesthetic norm, 'order in confusion'.

From Benlowes's 'choristae' come the 'winged Quires' which
'Echo about their tuned Fires'. Marvell had already combined
the senses in his description of the morning-walk, but there
potential beauty was lost in jejuneness of phrasing.

> Well shot ye Firemen! Oh how sweet,
> And round your equal Fires do meet;
> Whose shrill report no Ear can tell,
> But Ecchoes to the Eye and smell.

The other senses in their own way pick up inferences like
echoes of sounds in the garden too subtle to be heard. In
Novum Organum Bacon had written, 'we perceive that the
Flame of Fire-Arms is seen sooner than the Sound is heard,
although the ball must have struck the Air before the Flame,
which was behind it, could escape: the reason of which is, that
Light moves with greater Velocity than Sound'.[2] In that image
Marvell found an instance where the confusion of senses was
scientifically permissible. The application of the language belonging to one sense to another has a classical origin; but among

---

[1] *Theophila*, xii. 218, 'Argument'; but previously appearing in *Sphinx Theologia*
(*Praeludia*), p. 11, as 'Secessus, Animae Templum', and later, with variations, 'In
Praise of Oxford' (1673). See Røstvig, op. cit., pp. 247-8.
[2] II. xlvi.

the conceited writers of the Renaissance it found new favour, as a sort of catachresis, 'the expression of one matter by the name of another which is incompatible with it, and sometimes clean contrary', an abuse 'now in fashion'[1] in the 1590's. The materialization of sound was recognized as a particular example of this figure ('A voice beautiful to his ears').

> While in her blood they sitte with fierye wings
> Not vapord in her voyces stillerie,
> Nought are these notes her breast so sweetely frames
> But motions, fled out of her spirits flames.[2]

Like the song of Chapman's lady, Marvell's birds are too re-markable to be described in logical language. They are less substantial even than their music, which can be seen, while they are only heard. Herbert, and Vaughan after him, had described the movement of light in groups of verbs, such as 'hang and move', 'glitter, and curle, and winde', 'stream and flow', 'shine and move', 'work and wind'; and Vaughan had compared birds themselves to light.

> And now as fresh and chearful as the light
> Thy little heart in early hymns doth sing.[3]

But it is a description of 'The Nightingal' in *Partheneia Sacra* which further illuminates Marvell's meaning.

> But oh what sport it is, when this litle feathered voice, this pretty harmonie in the shape of a bird, this litle end of nothing, as it were, being vivifyed with musick, is even readie to kil herself with singing, when she heares the counterfet *Nightingal* (the Eccho) to mock her, in repeating and returning her whole melodie againe![4]

The idea of the echo as a 'counterfet' bird is further com-plicated, so that the bird itself becomes an echo to its own music, its 'tuned Fires', which burn centrally like altar-fires[5]

---

[1] John Hoskyns, *Directions for Speech and Style*, pp. 36–37, 'Synoeciosis'.
[2] *The Poems of George Chapman*, ed. cit., p. 60, 'Ovids Banquet of Sence'.
[3] From poems by Herbert and Vaughan called 'The Starre', and Vaughan, 'The Bird'.
[4] P. 142.
[5] One line of Benlowes runs 'Pectoris Ara Fides, Zelus Amorque Focus'.

in the sacred grove. A thought which would have been expressed by Vaughan in language dispersed, plain and energetic, becomes concentrated, mysterious, and thought-teasing in Marvell.

The life of the wood, in its order, its virtues and its failures, is an image of society. Nature shows its accustomed courtesy by setting high and low, the nightingale and the shrub, in musical consort. The stooping of the 'highest Oakes' is aristocratic; the 'listning Elders' respond in plebeian fashion, with the hint of a name-pun; the thorn shows the consideration due to a lady, and 'lest it should hurt her, draws / Within the Skin its shrunken claws'. Some birds appear in the wood for description's sake ('the hatching *Thrastles* shining Eye'); others have emblematic overtones, such as the doves and the 'Hewel' or wood-pecker. This bird, an ancient image of the devil in the human soul,[1] represents a wood-cutter in Drayton's poem *The Owle* ('The *Wood-pecker*, whose hardned beake hath broke / And peirc'd the heart of many a sollid Oke'). For Marvell the bird does not represent social evil; it is the fall of the tainted tree which it has 'mined' that reveals it. The oak, which stood popularly for kingship, is itself executed for harbouring the traitor-worm.

The poet's image of himself is a double one. He is lord of the wood, and at the same time so closely identified with non-human creatures that he becomes one of them. He is both '*easie Philosopher*', 'some great *Prelate of the Grove*', and bird or 'inverted Tree'. Yet this identity does not involve a decrease of intelligence: rather is he better able to understand their language.

> Already I begin to call
> In their most learned Original:
>
> .   .   .   .   .
>
> Out of these scatter'd *Sibyls* Leaves
> Strange *Prophecies* my Phancy weaves.

A poet like Vaughan was aware of his separation from the

---

[1] See *Physiologus*.

worship and jubilation of the creatures, but the paradox of
man's rule over the universe as Marvell expresses it is that man
comes closer to the creatures as he uses his power over them.
The poet is less of a Christian contemplator than some druid
or priest of nature. Like Davenant's Noah, who is humbled by
the flood to the level of the animals, he and the creatures are
'Joynt Tennants to the World, he not their Lord'. It seems
likely that he is related to a figure in Howell's poem, 'To the
knowing Reader',[1] which suggests that the druids were the
first British philosophers,

> So *calld*, because they commonly did use
> On God and Nature's works mongst *Trees* to muse,
> And fixe their Speculations; and in *rind*
> Of *Trees* was learning *swaddled* first, I find:
>
> . . . . .
>
> Then be not rash in censure, if I strive
> An ancient way of fancy to revive;
> While *Druyd* like conversing thus with *Trees*,
> Under their bloomy shade I Historize.
> *Trees* were ordaind for shadow, and I finde
> Their leafs were the first vestment of Mankinde.

The impression of unity among a diversity of things is
strengthened by the intertwining of bird and tree, so that 'the
Bird upon the Bough' behaves as 'if she were with Lime-twigs
knit', and the leafy oracles are compared to '*Plumes*'. They contain the wisdom of all ages, and their pattern of 'light *Mosaick*'
is emblematic of their prophetic character. The oak and the
ivy make for the poet the robes of his priesthood ('the first
vestment of Mankinde' in Howell's poem), and ally him with
the golden age. This '*Cope*' is both the forest itself and clerical
garb: it is both rustic and civilized. The modest prelacy of the
poet is intended as a contrast to 'Th'Ambition' of the '*Prelate
great*', the Archbishop of York, who had at one time been the
Fairfaxes' neighbour at Cawood.[2]

---

[1] See Howell, *Dodona's Grove, or The Vocall Forest* (1640–50).
[2] See stanza xlvi.

> Under this *antick Cope* I move
> Like some great *Prelate of the Grove*.

Marvell's conceits are saved from mere extravagance by a continual sense of place, so that even the most surprising image serves to build up the landscape because it springs directly from it as the only way of presenting some oddity of perception or another. Nature co-operates with the poet in his game of contemplation.

> And see how Chance's better Wit
> Could with a Mask my studies hit!

The preference hinted at here is for nature rather than art, but a nature rather different from the Mother of Regularity favoured by the Augustans. 'Chance' has something about it of the miracles of grace which come unexpectedly to men, also of the inspiration which arises on the spot as someone contemplates an object, 'the suddenness of a good Occasional Reflection'.[1] The poet has been engaged in serious meditation, and now the wood appears itself to be corroborating his surmises. (This may be in part a rejoinder to Davenant, who in his preface to *Gondibert* had preferred the wit of intelligence to the wit of chance.) 'Chance finisht that which Art could but begin.'[2]

VII

There are still other categories besides those of soldiery, travel, devotion to a lady, and pious contemplation by which Marvell measured the Nun Appleton estate. The 'Mask' provided by chance is both a veil and a dramatic performance, enacting the poet's thoughts and fulfilling them.

> No Scene that turns with Engines strange
> Does oftner then these Meadows change.

Both the formality of procession and dance ('the Triumphs of the Hay') and the continual modification of the landscape are conveyed through this kind of analogy.

---

[1] Boyle, *Occasional Reflections*, ed. cit., p. 38.
[2] Marvell, 'The last Instructions to a Painter', line 25, ed. cit., p. 141.

This *Scene* again withdrawing brings
A new and empty Face of things;

．　．　．　．　．

Then, to conclude these pleasant Acts,
Denton sets ope its *Cataracts*.

Some of Marvell's references to painting are simple, direct and contemporary. The meadow is 'as smooth and plain, / As Clothes for *Lilly* stretcht to stain'. On this empty space the poet then begins to sketch his landscape, recollecting as he does so the picture of the creation of the animals, 'th'Universal Heard', in Davenant's Temple of Praise.

They seem within the polisht Grass
A Landskip drawen in Looking-Glass.

Such comparisons with painting may be relatively trivial, but the poem has other finer relations with this art. The qualities which Marvell has discovered in his patron's estate are those valued by seventeenth-century theorists, 'sudden, quicke, and flickering light', 'an orderly and pleasant confusion', and 'a strange stealth of change'.[1] It is through the texture of his writing that Marvell suggests these qualities.

'Lanscape', wrote one of these instructors in the art of painting, 'is nothing but Deceptive visions, a kind of cousning or cheating your owne Eyes, by your owne consent and assistance.'[2] Marvell deceives through innumerable devices of his art, by sustaining an analogy until we believe in the absoluteness of its truth, by the interpenetration of different orders in a metaphor or in a pun, which places them in the strictest and most inviolable conjunction. By the operations of language, one thing has become another, and there is no gainsaying it. In extreme cases, one thing is turned into its opposite, war into peace, small to great, land to sea, man to creature, liquid to solid. Or opposite qualities are held in balance in a unifying

---

[1] Franciscus Junius, *The Painting of the Ancients* (1638), p. 278 and p. 281, quoting Zeuxis.

[2] Edward Norgate, *Miniatura*, ed. Martin Hardie (1919), p. 51. Daniel King, Mary Fairfax's tutor, made for her a treatise in MS. (B.M. Add. 12461), between 1653 and 1657, based heavily on Norgate.

wholeness of theme. 'The most contrary colours agree very well about the composition of an excellent beauty.'[1] (This is why it is inadequate to subject Marvell's poem to the anthologizing method, by which his intention to show how all things are included in Fairfax's estate is obscured.) There are other cases where the analogy is not between extremes, but still between things widely unlike; and there are others where one thing almost imperceptibly becomes another, or is mingled with another. In the terminology of painting this is 'Harmoge', the subtlety in shifting from one colour to another which has a delicacy 'like *spirits* and *souls* painted',[2] the 'thinne and misty Horizontal stroke' where sea and sky meet, when 'both are most strangely lost and confounded in our eyes, neither are wee able to discerne where the one or other doth begin or end: water and aire, severall and sundry coloured elements, seeme to be all one at their meeting'.[3] This is the kind of confusion which Marvell practised in the frequency of his use of the figure oxymoron, which leaves indistinct the bounds between things. The kingfisher is a '*Saphir-winged Mist*', the songs of birds are 'tuned Fires'. The perfumes of flowers are 'fragrant Vollyes' and their petals 'silken Ensigns'. The meadow is a 'green Sea', 'the Abbyss . . . Of that unfathomable Grass', the 'Grassy Deeps', and the wood 'this yet green, yet growing Ark'. Shadows on the water are '*Eben Shuts*', solid and immaterial at once. The poet himself is 'an inverted Tree' with a 'sliding Foot'; his fellow-men are 'rational *Amphibii*'.

Marvell was aware also of another way of producing illusions, by the use of the introductory phrase 'as if' and of the verb 'it seems'. The classical use of this construction is not witty on the whole, and only weakly metaphorical. By the time of the Renaissance its use was central to the presentation of landscape: it appears prolifically in Sidney's *Arcadia*, and Spenser found it to his purpose. It might create the impression that some inanimate object was alive and give a humanizing explanation

---

1 Junius, op. cit., p. 274, from Philostratus.
2 William Sanderson, *Graphice* (1658), pp. 47–49.
3 Junius, op. cit., p. 280.

for its behaviour (The good he numbers up, and hacks; / As if he mark'd them with the Ax', of the woodpecker), or it might introduce some personification as though it really existed. It might initiate a fairly simple simile ('The tawny Mowers enter next; / Who seem like *Israalites* to be'), or assist in the mistaking of one substance or thing for another (stanza lxiii illustrates this, with one 'seems' and two 'as if's'). The virtue of these words is that they tremble between the rather loose connexion of a common comparison and complete identity. Here is neither pure metaphor nor simile, but a shade between the two.

The landscape of 'Upon Appleton House' was intended to satisfy the taste of an age for which the doctrine of *ut pictura poesis* meant that both poetry and painting were emblematic, bodying forth important qualities and significances in attractive forms which both hid and expressed the truth. The strict description of nature and the power to distort in fidelity to the poetic vision had not split apart. The order of Marvell's landscape is hardly prosaic: it is an order in confusion which imitates the structure of the universe.

INDEX

PRINTED IN GREAT BRITAIN
AT THE UNIVERSITY PRESS, OXFORD
BY VIVIAN RIDLER
PRINTER TO THE UNIVERSITY